Popular
a memoir

VINTAGE WISDOM FOR A MODERN GEEK

MAYA VAN WAGENEN

DUTTON
AN IMPRINT OF PENGUIN GROUP (USA), LLC

B WAGENEN

DUTTON BOOKS

Published by the Penguin Group
Penguin Group (USA) LLC
375 Hudson Street | New York, New York 10014

USA | Canada | UK | Ireland | Australia
New Zealand | India | South Africa | China

penguin.com

A Penguin Random House Company

CIP Data is available

ISBN 978-0-525-42681-3

Printed in the United States of America

1 3 5 7 9 10 8 6 4 2

Designed by Danielle Calotta

To all those who've sat alone at the edge of the playground.
This book is for you.

Popular

a memoir

CONTENTS

· · · · · · · · · · · · · · · ·

Hi!

I'm Betty Cornell!

    I wrote Betty Cornell's Teen-Age Popularity Guide *in 1951. I was twenty-four. Pedal pushers were the hottest fashion trend. They hit just below the knee and were the shortest shorts around. Pleated skirts had hemlines that often fell to the ankle, and many girls knit crewneck sweaters themselves, which were all the rage. Miniskirts were still more than a decade away, and skinny jeans and crop tops were unheard of.*

    If you wanted a change for your hair, you got a reverse perm at the beauty salon. (There were no boxes of hair color at the drugstore, because no one dyed their hair!) To style my hair, each evening I would pin it up in rag curlers, stuffed with Kleenex to give more volume, go to bed, and wake up in the morning with the perfect pageboy hairstyle.

    But today, things have changed. I walk around town and see hair in hues of blues and pinks and the fashions are more revealing. While I have witnessed many fashion trends that were considerably less modest than what I wore growing up, I have been around long enough to recognize that a huge part of fashion is pushing the limits of the past. The more things have changed, it is interesting that the core motivation to outdo the previous generation clearly remains the same, just as it was when I wrote my book. It is comforting for me to know that even though I am no longer a prominent part of the fashion world, the end goal is still the same even if the product is not.

My most vivid memories of publishing my Teen-Age Popularity Guide are of how flattered I felt whenever I received letters from teenagers telling me how much they had learned by reading my book. They told me about their clothes, their hair, and their parties—I loved hearing from them.

However, I was surprised many years later by another letter my book brought me. And this time, it was by e-mail and turned out to be the most heartwarming and profound. It came from Maya Van Wagenen in April of 2012, and she told me that I had changed her life! She had used my book for tips and hints on how to deal with the challenges she was facing in school. Remarkably she used advice I wrote decades ago and applied it in today's world. I was so delighted to know that my book had withstood the test of time and was still providing help to teenagers.

When I finished reading Maya's book—this book you are about to read, too—I felt a cascade of feelings: pride, love, satisfaction, and happy memories. It amazed me to see Maya tell her tale with such knowledge, poise, and grace. Over the years, I have seen many good grooming and fashion trends *come and go and, on rare occasion, return years later with modifications to fit the new generation's taste. But I never thought when I was writing my book that the advice I offered would be made relevant sixty years later through the eyes of a new, young writer.*

I began my career as a model and then found great success as an author. Maya is starting her career as an author, but she is already a model of courage and confidence for her generation and generations to come.

Betty Cornell

Introduction

(or how this whole thing came to be)

"School is the armpit of life," my best friend Kenzie once told me. Amen. My school is no exception. Walk through the scratched glass doors on that first day and your life becomes a series of brutal and painful encounters: being called a dick by the football player who sits near you in science, standing in a bra and granny panties in front of your gym locker that you can't open while the girls around you giggle and point, crying in the bathroom because you didn't know it was possible for your heart to hurt this much. There is one thing, though, that can help you navigate this sweaty, smelly underarm, and that is a careful understanding of how the social food chain is organized.

MY SCHOOL'S POPULARITY SCALE
(From patricians to plebeians)

10. Volleyball Girls
9. Football Faction
8. Rich Gang Members (including More-Popular Girls Who Dress Seductively)
7. Band Geeks
6. Choir Geeks
5. Goth Art Chicks
4. Less-Popular Girls Who Dress Seductively
3. Pregnant Teens (We have two right now, a seventh and an eighth grader.)
2. Computer Geeks (There are hardly any.)
1. Library Nerds (who read constantly and love Japanese comics)
0. The Ignored (sixth graders)
− 1. Social Outcasts
− 2. Teachers
− 3. Substitute Teachers

You are categorized by where you spend your time and with whom you do, and do not, associate. I fall into the Social Outcast group, the lowest level of people at school who aren't paid to be there. I'm joined in my lowly negative-digit station by my close friend and confidant Kenzie. For the most part, it's a quiet, monotonous, invisible existence. That is, until you get noticed and preyed upon by someone in any of the tiers above you.

So how do those at the top work the class system to their advantage?

There are magazine articles and self-help books about what to wear, what to say, how to behave, and who to be friends with. In fact, long before I was even born, my father picked up a book at a thrift store. The faded cover was old and torn, but "There was something about it," he told me. He thumbed through the pages until he came upon the title: *Betty Cornell's Teen-Age Popularity Guide*. It was written in 1951, and was full of tips and advice on how to achieve what seemed to be the unachievable: improving one's social status. My dad said he found himself laughing right there in the store at some of the outdated ideas. It being an interesting piece of vintage pop culture, and he being my father, he bought it right away.

For a long time the book sat in his office (the "chamber of curiosities") at our house in Brownsville, Texas. It was gathering dust in a cardboard box sandwiched between a World War I helmet and a carved stone skull from some tribe in Mexico.

It was waiting to be discovered.

. . . .

As luck would have it, the book did not want to remain hidden. When my parents decided to clean out Dad's office (personally, I believe they made the whole mess angrier) Mom opened the box and rediscovered Betty Cornell's book. She wasn't sure what to do with it, so she handed it off to me, Maya, "Caretaker of All Stuff No One Wants, but Won't Get Rid Of."

I saw *Betty Cornell's Teen-Age Popularity Guide* as nothing more than a quirky book with advice along the lines of "Don't wear makeup on your eyes, instead use Vaseline," and "Close your pores with ice cubes," and "All girls should wear a girdle."

It was written by a former teen model who promised that, with a little hard work, poise, polish, and popularity were easily attainable for anyone.

Anyone?

I almost laughed.

That was when my mom had the idea—an amazing, terrifying, once-in-a-lifetime idea. "Maya, you should follow the advice this year, in eighth grade, and write about what happens."

My immediate answer was no. I couldn't imagine anything more horrifying. Since when had I (outwardly) cared about being popular anyway? But my mom planted a seed that day. Her comment was like one of those zits that starts out small, then gets really big and seems to never go away, no matter how many times you pop it.

A few days later, flipping through the book (yet again), I discovered this:

> *You will only make the situation worse if you take a negative attitude, if you shrug your shoulders and say, "Well, after all, who cares?" Basically somebody does care. You care. You care, because like everyone else on this planet you want to be liked, you want to be popular, you want to be a girl who gets around. You*

want to have a crowd to pal around with, a few
exciting dates, and at least one boy who thinks
you are about the most terrific female ever.
If you say that you don't, you are really only
fooling yourself. You are certainly not fooling
others.

The whole universe stood at attention.

Betty Cornell's book was published over sixty years ago, but somehow through the vast stretch of time and space, she saw what I secretly, desperately yearned for. More than that, she promised to help me get it.

I knew my life would never be the same.

. . . .

And so, I embark on my grand experiment. Every month of this school year I will follow Betty Cornell's advice on one of the topics in her book: dieting, hair, makeup, posture, and attitude, among others—no matter how embarrassing or complicated. I'll start with the easiest chapters first, the challenges that people won't notice right away. And then, month by month, I'll step it up, until I'm light-years away from my comfort zone.

I will take notes during the school day about reactions, thoughts, and anything else that happens. Upon returning home I will use those notes to help me remember the details and write about them in the most accurate way I possibly can. This is a fantastic literary exercise, and maybe it will help me to achieve my dreams of someday being an author. Hopefully journaling about the positive and negative things that happen will be empowering, showing that they are all part of a story that has begun to write itself. Maybe it will make it less scary.

I definitely have my work cut out for me. That is, if I'm not already beyond help. I am 5'2" with light brown skin that breaks out on a regular basis. I am gawky, slouchy, and just a little bit lumpy. I have nonexistent hips and a chest almost as flat as the cover of Betty Cornell's book. I wear glasses and braces. I do all my clothes shopping at Walmart and second-hand stores. I spend more time on algebra than I do on my hair.

Contents

My messy notes in Betty Cornell's Book

Sept. Figure Problems   May Dance Party/
October. Hair   PARTY!
November. Modeling Tricks
December. Makeup
January. Clothing
February. Good Grooming
March - Job
April - Popular Attitude

. . . .

I should probably take a moment to define what the word *popular* means as best I can. It's a complicated word. I know what it's not. It's not sitting alone, or being made fun of. It's not feeling ashamed of how you look and constantly wanting to hide in corners, wishing you could disappear. It's not what I feel right now.

Hopefully by the end of eighth grade, I will know what popularity is. But not only will I be able to define it, I will have experienced it.

Maybe things will change. Can popularity advice from more than half a century ago still be relevant? I'll find out. Crazier things have happened, right? Men have walked on the moon, and scientists have found a way to grow square watermelons.

For now, Betty Cornell has become my new soul mate, and I am married to her every word. For better or worse.

B.C. (Before Cornell)

September

FIGURE PROBLEMS

....

Nearly every teen has had . . . figure problems
at one time or another in her life. . . . The reason
this is so is that as a teen-ager your body is still
in a state of flux—it has not stopped growing
long enough to find its natural balance. . . . But
just because your body is restless and refuses to
settle down is no reason to despair of having a
good figure. It is a question of mind over matter.

I am average looking. Believe me, I'm not complaining. All my life, I've been more than happy to go unnoticed. When mean people forget I exist, the world is a much more cheerful place. But thanks to Betty, things are different. Now, I want to flourish, not just survive.

Ever since I was little, I've always had a *panza*, Spanish for belly. It's varied in size, but through the years it has been my constant companion. When I was in elementary school, my cousins used to poke my miniature muffin top, which usually led to me hiding in my room, crying, with a book and a chocolate bar. Obviously, bad habits start young.

I grew taller this past summer, prompting my *panza* to diminish a bit. It's wonderful to have my clothes fit better, but I am still painfully aware of my appearance and weight. I'm not alone in my suffering, though. I can't think of a single girl I know who is genuinely happy with her weight. The Volleyball Girls eat as little as is humanly possible, until there's hardly anything left of them. They'll publicly shame any member of the group who comes to school wearing skinny jeans that display the slightest hint of a dimple. "Valeria is fat! Valeria is fat!" they'll shout.

Outside of the top groups on the popularity scale, most people in my school are a little rounder. I think this accentuates the difference between those at the top and the bottom of the food chain. That is another reason why I've got to bid farewell to my *panza* for good. It can't come with me on my rise to the top.

Thursday, September 1

In preparation for this first month of my experiment, I open the faded book. I feel as though I'm embarking on a great sea voyage. As I slide my finger down the table of contents, I silently pray that it won't end up like the *Titanic*.

Spending time with Betty

I read the first chapter, "Figure Problems," and underline key points.

> 1. *Start by intelligently figuring out your*
>   *figure problem. Find out about your body.*

That isn't too hard. No hips, no breasts, no curves. Well, actually I have curves, but they start in the middle and go out.

> 2. *Always check first with your doctor*
>   *before you make plans to lose weight.*

This is no problem for me. A year ago, I visited a new pediatrician who told me that I was "bordering on the edge of obese." Her painful, inaccurate recommendation now gives me the permission I need to start a diet.

3.   *... it is just as important to count the calories you eat between meals as the ones you eat at meals. If fact, many of you would probably not need to diet if you cut down your between-meal nibbling.*

4.   *There is still to be considered all the gorging that takes place at parties, particularly at club meetings and general get-togethers.*

5.   *If you are serious about having a good figure, you must eat breakfast.*

6.   *... fried food of any sort is fattening.*

Okay, this is doable. Betty Cornell also includes possible menu ideas that I will definitely try. I'm going to give myself the weekend to indulge on contraband then start the diet on Tuesday morning, after Labor Day weekend. Fingers crossed!

Friday, September 2

I run for all I'm worth. The bus home could leave any second, and I'm not on it. It's well over 90 degrees out, and already unsightly sweat stains are blossoming under my arms. Lovely.

One of the security personnel outside the school yells at me, but I ignore him. Since we live on the Texas/Mexico border, they're just here to make sure that no one is smuggling drugs. Which I'm not. I see Kenzie raise her eyebrows at me through one of the bus's dirty windows. The bus driver seems reluctant to open the door and mumbles something in

Spanish when I get on, panting uncontrollably. Some of the sixth graders snicker.

"Wow, you look like an idiot."

"Hi, Kenzie," I manage. I sink into the seat behind her and attempt to smooth back my frazzled ponytail.

"Why were you running?" She spits out the last word. Kenzie is half-Korean, with a wild personality, curly hair, a passion for heavy metal, and a hearty disdain for most exercise.

"We had to get sized for our performance gowns in choir." Ms. Charles, our director, had spent the whole time guessing our dress sizes and announcing them in her microphone. Her guess for me was way too big. I wonder if that should tell me something.

"Yet another reason I'm grateful not to be in that hell-hole," Kenzie snorts. She's been in band since sixth grade. She plays the oboe, but she doesn't have her instrument with her today, because she "accidentally" dropped it in the hallway, and it "like, um, kind-uh, sort-uh" broke.

I first met Kenzie two years ago on the first day of school. She was sitting alone, wearing a studded belt, and her frizzy hair was pulled back into a menacing ponytail. All I could think was, "Gosh, I hope she doesn't kill me." Little by little our classes forced us together and we soon became close, although it's clear that she could still take me out in a fight. She's really cool despite her dark aura. She's my opposite in every way, but she's one of the few people who doesn't make me feel like an outsider.

Seeing my Hispanic facial features but light skin, kids here ask if I'm Mexican. I answer that my mom is half, so that makes me a quarter. Actually my mother is a mix of English,

French, Spanish, Jewish, Mexican Indian, and African. I'm not sure how you classify that, but on her it's beautiful. For me, in a school district that is 98 percent Hispanic, I'm told that I don't have enough of the right DNA to be part of team-Latino. Ironically, off the border, I consider myself Mexican.

Maybe with Kenzie being Korean, me not being Mexican enough, and neither of us with sufficient knowledge of Spanish to ask directions to a bathroom, we connected by not fitting in anywhere else.

Although Kenzie isn't the pillow-fight-at-sleepovers type, I've always appreciated her honesty. If I have a booger in my nose, she tells me. If my fly is down, she's quick to let me know.

"Maya," she says now, "you're a mess. Like, really."

Friends like that are hard to find.

The sixth graders are staring at us over the tops of the seats with large eyes. "They look so innocent," I say. They giggle in their prepubescent voices.

"Not for long," Kenzie grins. She turns to them and shame-lessly belts out a chorus of filth that includes the anatomically correct names of body parts and their biological functions.

I hide my face in my hands. I try to chastise her, but Kenzie is laughing so hard, she can't hear anything.

Just before we get to my stop, one of the sixth graders turns around and spits at me.

First week of school down, countless more to go.

And yet, this year will be different. This year I have a plan.

. . . .

I open the front door.

"Hi, babe!" Mom chimes from the kitchen. To my surprise there is a box of apple fritters on the counter. I notice the perky yellow *60 percent off* sticker. I also see a bag of stale cookies and a loaf of cinnamon raisin bread. They all have the yellow tag. And a massive calorie count.

"I shopped without eating breakfast," Mom says. "I hear that it has an effect on what you buy."

I nod solemnly.

"But don't worry," she continues, "it was all on clearance."

Mom has a not-so-secret love affair with food. "It could be worse," she says. "I could be a raging alcoholic or a cocaine addict." Mostly she buys chocolate. When I was little, I used to find her stashes of sweets. They were always in places where my dad would never think to check, like the cleaning closet or the vegetable drawer. But Mom works out at the gym Monday through Friday and is rather fit.

"How was your day?" she asks.

I look down at my feet. "I got spit on by a sixth grader."

She bites her lip respectfully to keep from laughing. "I guess it's a good thing that it's the weekend, huh?"

I nod and grab a fritter out of the package. Natalia, my autistic five-year-old sister, wanders in with crumbs all over her face. It's quite clear that she's already enjoyed hers.

"Eat quickly, Maya," Mom says. "Those have to be gone by the time your father gets home."

. . . .

Dad opens the door an hour or so later. He throws out his arms in a gesture of defeat and shouts, "Well, we're officially the Fat Wagenens!" It's definitely not his usual "Hello, everyone!" or "I missed you all." He must have had a rough day. The university is really struggling, and they're getting ready to fire faculty.

"Excuse me?" Mom's voice rings out loud and clear.

My nine-year-old brother, Brodie, cowers in the doorway, a banana grasped in his hand. His eyes are wide. He's rather touchy about his size, and how quickly he's growing out of his clothes. He's most often prey to Dad's "You-know-(Insert-Name-Here)-the-eating-habits-that-you-develop-as-a-child-stay-with-you-your-whole-life," lectures.

"I said we are officially the Fat Wagenens. I saw the doctor today and he said that I have to lose some weight. We all need to lose some weight."

"Excuse me?!" Mom is really quite angry now. She has that dangerous tone in her voice she sometimes gets when she's on the edge. Dad's weight plan can only mean three people in our family. Like I said, Mom works out, and Natalia never stops moving, so her calves are like rocks.

I go upstairs to avoid seeing Mom and Dad whisper-fight. Brodie is staring wide-eyed at his *panza*.

"Oh please," I say. "You're just going through a chubby stage. I did too when I was nine." I don't mention that mine hasn't ended yet, but it's okay to bend the truth when trying to build self-esteem.

He smiles halfheartedly.

Maybe it's a good thing that I'm starting the Betty Cornell Diet on Tuesday. It sure would make Dad happy. Anyway, I'm not ready to start signing my name Maya "Fat" Wagenen.

Monday, September 5

Many of you bring your lunches to school and buy milk at the cafeteria. That is a good way to avoid temptation—you don't even have to go near the long line of delicious dishes. . . . Any sensible combination of three or four of these items will make a healthful luncheon and probably one that is light and easy to carry. . . .

1. *Hard-boiled eggs.*
2. *Small container of cottage cheese.*
3. *One slice of whole-wheat or rye bread . . .*
4. *Fresh fruit (you can eat lots of it).*
5. *American or Swiss cheese sandwich, lots of lettuce—no mayonnaise—use whole-wheat or rye bread.*
6. *Any kind of lean meat sandwich.*
7. *Consommé.*
8. *Milk.*

I pack a lunch of a half sandwich, some applesauce, and a hard-boiled egg. I don't include any meat though, because I've been a vegetarian since I was eight years old, thanks to *Charlotte's Web*, my pet parakeet, and a bad case of the stomach flu.

I'm feeling rather conflicted about starting my diet tomorrow. While I'm excited about the prospect of losing weight, I'm sad to say good-bye to carefree eating. Let's hope everything goes well!

Tuesday, September 6

It's funny how we live on the southernmost border of the United States, the epicenter of fantastic Mexican cuisine, and yet the school serves frightfully below-average cafeteria meals. Our town is a land of contradictions.

Ironically, like me, Brownsville, Texas, is a place that doesn't quite fit into any category. It's not quite the United States, and it's not quite Mexico. My father got a job here at the university the summer before my sixth-grade year. So we moved from the West to this place Brodie fondly describes as "The gum stuck to the bottom of the shoe of the U.S." Our school is across the street from the poorest community of its size in the nation. Down the road is a *raspa* (snow cone) stand, a *panadería* (bakery), a very shady-looking doctor's office, a taco place, and a used tire shop.

But the food makes up for everything. Even as a vegetarian in the land of fajitas, I never run out of vibrant flavors and colors to experience. Granted not everything's enticing. In the meat section of the grocery store, you can buy pig heads and chicken feet. Dad says there's even a way to make intestines taste good (in tacos, in case you're wondering). If such a deed can be accomplished, then there should be a way to make the school lunches look and smell less like melted plastic.

These are the days I'm grateful to bring my own lunch. While I nibble on some carrot sticks, curvy and voluptuous Kenzie eats two jumbo chocolate chip cookies, the same as every day. Oh, how I envy her. I try to keep in mind what Betty says.

> *If the prospect of lunch without a sweet dessert is too gruesome for you to imagine, there's no hope for you. You have allowed your sweet tooth to overrule your wisdom tooth. . . . As for taunts from your friends—and they will taunt you—keep your chin up and your weight down.*

Wednesday, September 7

Kenzie and I walk to the library—"the Fishbowl" as we call it—in the morning. The library gets its nickname from its three glass walls. We volunteer there in the mornings and during lunch as an escape from the cruelty of the outside world. Our librarian, Ms. Corbeil, is one of a kind. She welcomes all Social Outcasts and talks to us like we're adults and worthy of her attention, something many of us don't get very often. She's funny, smart, and rides a motorcycle. Teachers come to her to talk about anything from faulty technology equipment to a midlife crisis. And she buys new books with her own money because the school cut almost all of her budget. So it's no wonder that the Fishbowl is an oasis, a home away from home.

On our way, we pass Mr. Lawrence as he limps down the hall. He catches my eye and smiles.

"Hi, Maya, how's everything going? I sure do miss having you in my class this year."

I stop. "I miss having you as a teacher!"

I met Mr. Lawrence in sixth grade when he was in charge of the school's literary club. When I showed up at his room for the first meeting, he asked me if I liked to write. I told him, "More than anything."

Mr. Lawrence and me in sixth grade

He submitted my stories and poems to competitions and the local newspaper. He pushed me to enter every contest that came up, and would e-mail the people in charge for weeks to find out if I placed. Although I didn't always win, he was proud of me. He read my work to all his classes, to the other teachers, to anyone who'd listen. He's the best teacher I've ever had. But he's getting older, and I can tell by his tired eyes and the way that he walks (now with a cane) that he's going to have to retire soon. The thought makes me want to cry.

Friday, September 9

If you are one of those Lazy Lils who just can't get up in time to eat breakfast, then you are starting the day off on the wrong foot. . . . Eating a good breakfast may not come easily at first. But after a little practice you'll enjoy it. . . . And you'll feel much better for doing so.

Government statistics show that 96 percent of the students in my district are "economically disadvantaged." Therefore, everyone is provided breakfast and lunch for free, whether you ask for it or not. In the past we've eaten both meals in the cafeteria, but this year the district has decided to serve breakfast in our classrooms. They say that it's to ensure that we get a healthy start to our day, but it's hard to believe that when you see what they bring in.

The breakfasts are packages of sugar-sweetened cereal, chocolate milk, and some sort of fried meat-filled thing— Betty Cornell definitely would not approve. I eat some whole-wheat toast and fruit as my classmates gorge on Lucky Charms. I stopped eating those things years ago when they turned Brodie's poop neon green, scaring the living daylights out of my parents.

After breakfast, our reading class goes to the Fishbowl. I lend a hand by helping my classmates check out books. I almost feel popular.

And then, of course, Carlos Sanchez, leader of the Football Faction swaggers up with a devious grin on his face. He's a tall, scrappy-looking jock. His short, dark brown hair is slicked forward in an attempt to make him look cool.

He hands me a skinny picture book about race cars and a novel called *Gay-Neck*, a Newbery Award Winner with a bird on the cover.

"I like cars," he says, as if that explains everything. "And this is a book about gay pigeons."

"Hmmm." I bite back what I really want to say which is, "Gee, Carlos Sanchez, I didn't know you had such an interest in homosexual wildlife." Instead I hand him the books and mutter that they're due on the twenty-third.

He goes off to the corner with his football cronies who laugh at his every pitiful joke. "Hey, guys, it's about a gay pigeon."

Our reading teacher gives him the death stare over her glasses. She's got it down to a science.

"I mean gay as happy, you know, like emotions and stuff," he adds quickly, sheepishly looking down at his fancy sneakers.

Remind me again how he got to be popular.

. . . .

In addition to sharing Betty Cornell's wisdom on how to not just survive, but thrive, at school, I've decided to pass along my own insights that I pick up along the way.

> *Maya's Popularity Tip*
>
> When one of your peers has an interest in gay pigeons, it is best to hold your tongue—even when you'd rather come up with a snarky comment—especially when no one but the books are around to applaud your wit.

. . . .

We're on our way to the beach this evening. I'm wedged in the backseat between Brodie, who sits drawing monsters and weapons of mass destruction in a notebook, and Natalia, who is clicking her tongue and reciting songs from *Blue's Clues*.

When we get to the beach, we all take long deep breaths of the salty South Padre Island air. We've been here five minutes, and I'm already feeling bad about my body and how I look in a bathing suit. *"Now overweight is nothing to be alarmed about. It is easy enough to do something about it and do something about it sensibly,"* Betty says.

I know, I know. So far I've been slowly cutting back on my eating, but I haven't lost any weight.

I look down at my one-piece. It's the first one I've ever owned with actual breast padding. It's nice because it makes my 34A boobs look just a little bit perkier.

Natalia is giving me a goofy grin while Mom tries to get her into a bathing suit. "Smile!" she says. I lean down so she can rub her face in my ponytail.

Uh-oh. Natalia has taken off running down the beach.

Did I say running?

I mean sprinting.

Did I mention that she's completely naked?

Sunday, September 11

Church today. I have to listen to Mrs. Garcia talk again about how marriage to a man of our faith is the one thing that girls our age need to be planning for. We can always "learn more things as a mom than from going to college."

I try not to listen too closely.

I see Ethan, my darling crush, sitting on the other side of the chapel. I sigh and for the first time, I really wish that this diet was working.

He really has the most gorgeous eyes.

And hair.

And smile.

I wonder if the boys Betty Cornell crushed on all liked her back.

He catches me staring at him.

He raises his beautiful eyebrows at me and mouths the words, *What are you looking at?*

I hide my burning face and say a silent prayer of gratitude that he didn't catch me drooling this time.

I only ate a light breakfast before leaving, and now my stomach is bellowing like a horny walrus. It's bad.

> ~~~ *Maya's Popularity Tip* ~~~
> If your stomach is prone to making
> loud noises when your crush is within earshot,
> seriously consider having it removed. It will
> save you tons of embarrassment.

. . . .

In her book, Betty Cornell gives some instructions on how to do certain exercises that help maintain a well-balanced figure.

> *Now to flatten the tummy, resorting . . . to the
> boys' football practice. Lie on the floor and raise
> the feet to a 45-degree angle; now lower them,
> keeping the knees straight, ever so slowly to the
> count of ten. Feel it pull? Although I know this
> exercise hurts, it also helps.*

Once you get the hang of her exercises they're easy as pie. Sort of.

Yum.

Pie.

Trying but not quite succeeding at Betty's exercises

. . . .

Tuesday, September 13

I've lost a whole six-tenths of a pound!

The diet is working.

Will anyone notice? More specifically, will Ethan notice?

Other good news. My bra is officially too tight! I never thought it would happen because I come from a long line of small-breasted women. But every time I put it on it cuts off my circulation.

I'm so full of happiness and hormonal-ness that I can hardly stand it. So just for fun I tried on Mom's bra, which is the next size up.

I don't even begin to fill it.

I am greatly humbled.

I'm still doing the Betty Cornell exercises, but I haven't yet made the promised transformation from *"tubby teen"* to *"the girl with the well-proportioned figure."* I'll keep it up, though, because it's not over until the fat lady sings. Ha-ha-ha.

Thursday, September 15

In PE, Kenzie and I are sweaty, exhausted, and our arms are bruised from spiking rock-hard volleyballs. Ever since I started "Figure Problems," I've made an effort to become better at one sport. I've never been remotely coordinated, and I have the knees of a seventy-year-old woman. It's quite embarrassing to give PE my all and still be so terrible at everything I try. It's intimidating to know that the top of the social hierarchy is based on athletic ability. It feels so ancient, so raw. The strong survive. The weak get eaten. Betty doesn't have any quick fixes to suddenly gain years of athletic experience, skill, and strength in a month. I looked.

Kenzie and I crowd around the locker we share. It's like having a roommate whose only possessions are deodorant and sweaty gym shorts.

"Wow, I stink," Kenzie blurts.

I laugh.

"No, I'm serious," she says. "Here, smell my shirt." She wipes the perspiration off her face using a sleeve, and hands it to me.

"Ew. I'm not going to sniff your shirt. And you just made your face smell like phys. ed."

"Smell it!"

"Look, Kenzie. As friends, there are things that we share, like lockers and an occasional uncomfortable secret, but I refuse to smell your shirt. That takes things a little too far."

"Oh."

Maya's Popularity Tip

If you want to be popular, don't go around smelling people's PE clothes, otherwise you will be labeled a creep and you will be forced to change in the bathroom stalls.

. . . .

Saturday, September 17

Today we're going to the *pulga* (flea market). We pull into the parking lot, a large expanse of windblown dirt on the side of the freeway. Dad and Brodie love coming to the *pulga* because they're treasure hunters. I enjoy coming too because I get to be with Dad. He spends so much time on campus these days, I hardly ever see him. I take his hand as we walk to the first row of stands.

Pulga *entrance*

Mom describes the *pulga* as the world's biggest Mexican yard sale. I'd have to agree. Many people in Brownsville who come over the border illegally can't get jobs, so they sell things at the *pulga*, including stuff they find on the side of the road. We've saved ourselves many trips to the dump by simply dragging large, unwanted possessions out to the curb at night.

Like magic, they're gone by sunrise.

At the *pulga* are shoes, used toys, clothes, antiques, electronics, plants, tools, religious statues, candles, and mystical remedies. Once we even saw a piano, just sitting there in the dust. It made Mom cry.

There's a ton of food, too. A van that only sells mayonnaise and *chile*-coated corn on a stick. *Elote entero.* Oh yeah, it exists. There are potatoes that are spiral sliced, fried, and served on a long wooden stick. I would eat one, but we once saw a vendor fish the rods out of the trash to reuse them. There's also a soup made out of cow stomach and old men who wander around with carts full of ice cream—*paletas.*

People in the stalls shout, "*Pásale, pásale!*" which means "Pass through here!" There are great jugs of *aguas* (juices) sweating in the heat, and tables overflowing with exotic vegetables and fruits. There are cacti and palm trees, chickens, turtles, parakeets, and doves—all for sale.

As Brodie and I stop at a stand with rats and iguanas in rusty cages, Dad grabs our hands and drags us away.

"What?" Brodie asks, angrily. "Why are we leaving? I'm not done!"

"Shhh." Dad takes us down another row before he explains.

"Sorry, two guys with shaved heads and tattoos were making plans for a drug deal. I thought it would be best to get out of there."

I nod. I'm beyond being shocked anymore.

We make our way to the *raspa* stand. A *raspa* is a Mexican snow cone except ten times better than those syrupy messes in flimsy paper cups. There's a *raspa* stand down the street from my school, but I'm kind of afraid to go there because that's where all the fights happen.

Dad looks around. "You can buy a casket, hire a lawyer, and select your fresh produce all at the same place," he says wistfully. "You should remember all this. We're not going to be here forever, you know."

I smile as we eat our *raspas* and listen to the ubiquitous *ranchera* music and the bustle of people passing by.

Eating raspas

. . . .

Wednesday, September 21

I had a dream last night that a television show host came to our house and poured just-add-water potato flakes into the washing machine. He put it on the spin cycle and whipped up a massive load of mashed potatoes. I woke up just as I was trying to convince him not to put them in the dryer.

I think this diet is messing with my head.

On the bright side, I've lost two whole pounds so far!

Monday, September 26

Ugh. I am so sick. I spent all of last night extremely nauseous. I'm still at school, though, trying to keep in mind my fourth popularity tip.

Maya's Popularity Tip

Never throw up in class. It's better just to run out of the room and retch in the hallway. Even if you make it to the trash can in the corner, if anyone sees you puke, you will be tormented forever. During elementary school I hurled in a wastebasket. When we moved away five years later, the last thing one boy said to me was, "You're that girl who barfed in kindergarten." It's impossible to live some things down.

I'm skipping lunch and heading straight to the library.

Ms. Corbeil waves from behind the circulation desk where she's preparing some of the new books she bought to go on the shelves. There are a lot, and all are hardcover, so I know they were expensive. But I don't say anything. We both know that for a lot of kids this library is the only place they can read new books. Many of them can't afford the luxury of newly released, much anticipated novels. The hold list for these new titles is already a mile long, so she's happy to be generous.

I grab a stack of books off the "Check In" cart and begin shelving.

"Oh, hi, Maya," I hear Leon say as he pushes his glasses up his nose. Leon is a sweet boy who was in my Technology class last year. I was the only one who would talk to him because he's a little different.

"Hi, Leon."

"You look beautiful today, Maya, absolutely fabulous!"

"Thank you, Leon." All the other girls would giggle and run away whenever Leon told them how pretty they were. I don't mind. In fact, I enjoy it. Hearing someone tell me honestly that I look good makes my day brighter.

Tuesday, September 27

As I am doing my Betty Cornell exercises, I hear Brodie pounding on his drum pad downstairs. Mom, Dad, and Brodie dress up in American uniforms from the U.S.-Mexican War of 1846 and participate in the living history program at the nearby Palo Alto Battlefield. It's just as nerdy as it sounds. Brodie is the drummer boy and Mom plays the fife. Dad dresses up just so he can shoot the cannon. I stay home and babysit Nat so they can spend all day under the boiling hot sun in their wool uniforms. I am not jealous at all.

If you haven't guessed yet, my family is made up of ultra-nerds. This is not necessarily a bad thing. We play games like Scrabble and watch documentaries together. I have always known that I am going to college. Yet, there are times when it can get a little embarrassing. As Mom admits, "Re-enacting is the final step before *Star Trek* conventions." In a couple of years, my family will probably be doing that, too.

Dad and Brodie at Palo Alto Battlefield

. . . .

Friday, September 30

Today is the last official day of my diet, and I have lost three pounds this past month. It's not spectacular, but it's something. Although from now on I have to watch what I eat, I get to relax a little and enjoy myself. I think Betty Cornell would be proud.

I'm walking down the hall with Kenzie.

"Kenzie," I say, after she finishes venting about her last class. "What makes someone popular?"

She places her hands on my shoulders and stares at me. Her eyes burrow deep into mine, as if she's preparing to bestow upon me great wisdom.

"How the hell should I know?"

The final bell rings, and I hurry off to the bus in thoughtful silence.

"Hey, you there," I hear someone shout behind me. At first I think it's a girl, but a quick scanning of the crowd reveals that it's actually a really short sixth-grade boy. He smiles at his Munchkin Guild and then walks over to me.

Oh no, he's going to ask for my number. What should I say?

I can't say no or else I may break his itty-bitty heart.

But if I say yes, then I will be known as the "stupid moron who was idiotic enough to give an Oompa Loompa her phone number."

I already have a boy I like. His name is Ethan. He even knows my name.

I guess I'll just have to politely refuse and run away.

He looks up at me with a big grin and says, "My friend just called you a *Fat Ugly Nerd*."

Really?

Really.

Do the Popularity gods hate my (obviously overweight) guts? Am I really going to have to spend the rest of the school year being called plump by garden gnomes who think that it's cool to make milk come out their noses?

But in spite of the ridicule, I have lost weight. My clothes fit me better, and all in all, I feel good about what I've accomplished. Still, there's so much left to do.

I know, Betty, chin up, weight down.

October

HAIR

....

Beautiful hair is about the most important thing
a girl has. . . . pretty hair can always overcome
the handicap of a not-so-pretty face. . . . Your hair
can make you or break you.

My straight, dark brown hair is thick and grows very quickly.
I've never had bangs because of the extremely bad ancestral
cowlicks that run so deeply in my DNA. Although I'm not
picky about how my locks are styled, I can't stand it when
they're down and touching my neck or face. That's a challenge
I need to face this month. I usually have long hair that reaches
down my back, but over the summer Mom took me to get it
cut by someone a friend knew instead of the usual cheap chain
salon (Dad noticed they didn't sterilize their equipment).

Anyway, the woman only spoke Spanish and Mom struggled to explain the length I wanted. Needless to say, I came home with much shorter hair than I'd intended. Now it's about shoulder length and my ponytail is only five inches. I don't mind it, though. It makes for less effort in the styling department.

My fashion statement for the last two years has been a low, messy ponytail with pencils jabbed through it. Volleyball Girls and members of the Football Faction have been known to steal them without my knowledge.

I know. It's sad.

Betty Cornell says, *"If you keep your hair healthy, if you change the style often enough, you can count on it that you will be known as a girl with beautiful hair."*

I'm shaking like a leaf, I'm so nervous. I sure hope she's right.

Saturday, October 1

This is the first meeting of the NJHS (National Junior Honor Society, a service group that I joined because it will look good on my college application), and Mom is driving me.

"You look so cute," she says.

"I don't want to hear it."

"No, really, you're adorable!"

"Shut it," I beg.

Mom smiles at me and I glare a hole through the dashboard. We're stuck behind an old woman with Mexico license plates who's going twenty miles under the speed limit.

"GO!" Mom yells. She has this funny way of shouting at

people so that no one outside the car can tell that she's angry. She grins at them and speaks without moving her mouth. I personally think that she'd make an amazing ventriloquist.

Finally, we pull up to the public library where the meeting is being held. She kisses me on the top of my parted head. "Have fun!" she says, and drives away in her minivan. I walk toward the double doors and see some NJHS members are waiting outside for their friends to arrive.

"Wow, Maya. Pigtails. Wow." A girl with her hair perfectly rolling down her shoulders stifles a laugh.

Don't let yourself become a fuddy-duddy about fashion. Don't stick to a pompadour when it has gone out of style. Don't keep on wearing your hair the same old way, when the passé styles make you look old hat.

I wince as she starts giggling and pulling on the two stubby growths sticking out the sides of my head.

Maya's Popularity Tip

When you're wearing an embarrassing hairstyle and people have started to notice, it's always safest to have a sudden, urgent, need to pee.

I immediately make a beeline toward the bathroom, and from there escape to the children's section of the library where the other students are waiting. We're helping with Hispanic Heritage Month activities. I recognize Catalina from choir and walk toward her. She's trying to make an 1840s Mexican soldier hat, but the black construction paper contraption more closely resembles an upside-down ice-cream cone.

"I like your pigtails, Maya."

"Thanks."

"Wanna go outside and try to convince people to come in and make hats and crafts and stuff?"

I nod and make my own hat. It's a lot harder than it looks. I finally get it to hold together but find that it won't fit over my head because of my pigtails. *Aw man, I guess I've got to take one for the team.* I gleefully pull down my carefully planned hairstyle and slide my hat on. Catalina and I walk outside.

"Nice dunce caps," an old man shouts as he walks through the door.

I won't even try to contradict this statement. Maybe it's because my dunce cap has slipped down over my eyes and I am momentarily blinded.

Monday, October 3

"Well, it seems that after years of being Maya, you've finally dropped the stupid ponytail." The girl behind me in algebra sneers. "Just look at you with your hair down."

I guess this girl proves Betty Cornell's statement true, *"Hair . . . is what we remember most about a person."*

At my school, most girls wear their hair down; boys use gel and style a small ridge toward the front of their heads (it's actually quite comical). How your hair looks is generally a good indicator of your place on the popularity scale. Those with the messiest hair are at the bottom. Those who spend hours on the appearance of their "do" are at the top. I think the longest I've ever spent on my hair is five minutes, if that tells you anything. When someone puts more effort into their hairstyle, it automatically shows that they are looking to increase their status. This feeble plea for recognition seldom goes unnoticed. In fact, most people overflow with compliments until the new hairstyle gradually becomes part of their identity.

I smile and nod at the girl behind me, whose comment I've decide to take as a flattering remark. It's hard to focus, though, because I'm about ready to explode. I can hardly stand the tickle of hair on the back of my neck. I try to listen to the teacher.

"Now, class, we're going to be called into an assembly about student conduct."

The girl behind me continues playing with my hair, patronizingly petting me like some mange-ridden hamster.

"So, will all people with the last names N–Z kindly walk to the auditorium?"

I get up with all the Nuñezes, Sanchezes, and Vasquezes. We shuffle to the cafeteria, which the teachers all call the auditorium because it sounds a lot fancier than "the big, funny-smelling room with ugly green-and-white tile and strange food spots all over." I look for somewhere to sit and I see Catalina. As I walk over to her, a member of the Football Faction crashes into me, and I lose my balance. I stumble onto the bench next to Catalina only to fall over backward. Fortunately my foot-and-a-half thick backpack breaks my fall. And Mom says that I should stop carrying so much.

"Oh my GOSH! Maya are you okay?"

I smile from my spot on the ground and murmur, "Just fine." I heave myself up, already knowing I'm going to be bruised.

But by this time, Catalina has moved on and is talking with some of her other friends.

I smooth down my hair. There's no way I can be popular with hair like a wild woman. *Ooh, that sounds like Betty Cornell. Maybe I'm starting to channel her essence in my day-to-day life.* I run my fingers through it and I notice there's a dried-up chunk of food nestled there. Ewww.

The assistant principal waves his arms, signaling for us to quiet down so that he can start. He lumbers to the front of the room and begins his slide presentation in a monotone voice. He goes on and on about our uniforms: a yellow polo shirt with a white undershirt (any other color might promote gang violence). Then he changes to a slide titled "Hair."

HAIR

- There will be no distracting hairstyles because they promote gang violence.
- There will be no distracting hair colors because they promote gang violence.
- All facial hair must be shaved because it promotes gang violence (a few mustached gang-bangers in the back are visibly angry about this).
- No bandannas will be allowed because they promote gang violence.

He goes on: "No body piercings will be allowed, other than on your ears. Because they promote gang violence."

"What if they're on parts of your body that no one sees?" Carlos Sanchez yells out. I hide my face. Really? But he looks like he's actually serious.

The assistant principal just shakes his head and clicks to the next slide.

HORSEPLAY

- No pushing
- No shoving
- No hitting
- No wrestling
- No fights on school property
- All of the above promote gang violence.

"Sir! Sir! What if it's not on school property?" Carlos Sanchez yells, jumping up and down.

"Like I said, we can't really do anything about that."

Carlos Sanchez stands on the table and pumps his fist in the air, "Woo-hoo! *Raspa* stand after school! *Raspa* stand after school!"

There is a chorus of boneheads who all shout in agreement. The teachers don't even try to reign in the chaos, but instead just wait the remaining few minutes until the bell rings and dismiss us to our classes.

Tuesday, October 4

In an attempt to boost school spirit, it's "Crazy Hair Day" today, but I've decided to just wear my hair in low pigtails instead of something outrageous. I wouldn't want to promote gang violence.

After the bell for third period rings, I escape to the library. Two students are sitting at a table. They look like troll dolls with their blue-and-orange hair standing up in the air. They are talking about someone from our campus who's recently been "relocated" to the alternative school for "troubled kids." In my computer class last year I sat next to a new kid who'd transferred from there. He was rough looking with short, uneven hair, like the barber who trimmed it was drunk. His name was Miguel, but I secretly called him "Motormouth" because he never stopped talking. He told me that he'd been arrested three times, that his life was pretty much a boring waste of time, and that the best place to hide marijuana was in the heel of high-top sneakers. He was sent back to the alternative school one week later.

After he left, the police came to school with drug dogs. They had our class (fourth-period Technology) leave our stuff in the room and line up against the wall in the hallway. The dogs were directed to smell each one of us and our bags.

Coincidence? There's no such thing.

Maya's Popularity Tip

When the boy sitting next to you in class kindly informs you that the best place to hide pot is in the heel of high-top shoes, you might want to think twice about wearing that style. You don't want to give people the wrong impression.

Thursday, October 6

When it comes to shampooing your own hair,
plan to save at least one night a week for the job.
Most teens prefer Thursday night because it puts
their hair in shape for the week-end.

It's Thursday so I grab shampoo and conditioner out of the bathroom cabinet. They're called Strawberry-Tangerine Smoothie. I personally don't want my hair to smell like dessert, but it's the only thing I can find.

Begin your shampoo by brushing your hair
thoroughly. Then tub your head well in water, apply
the shampoo, and scrub. Work up a good lather
and make sure that it penetrates every square inch.
Now rinse out the first lather and start afresh. With
the second lathering you should have removed all
the dirt. Then rinse your hair three times. With the
third rinsing, you should hear the hair squeak as it
runs through your fingers.

When I finish, Mom helps me by putting my hair in rag curlers, which Betty recommends for long hair, because they *"will not split the ends, and they are lots more comfortable to sleep on."*

"Wow, your hair isn't greasy at all," she says, wrapping my squeaky-clean tresses in the curlers.

"I would hope not," I say. She smiles.

I lean my head against her knee. She has to sit on a chair to do my hair because I'm as tall as she is now. Growing up is strange. When I was little, I couldn't wait to get older. Now I'm not so sure. It's hard realizing that your hand is larger than your mother's. It makes me sad.

"You look just like those girls on *Little House on the Prairie* with your hair like that. You're so adorable."

I groan. Adorable isn't popular. Adorable is what you call a Chihuahua that gets carried around in a purse.

I tell Mom this. She laughs, gives me a hug, and assures me that I don't look like a handbag dog. She always knows what to say.

My rag curlers

Friday, October 7

I wake up early so I can take the curlers out of my hair.

I slowly unroll them, twenty-four in all, and see that they've made little ringlets all over my head.

OH NO! I LOOK LIKE A BROWN-ISH SHIRLEY TEMPLE!

I can't go to school today, I just can't.

. . . .

At school.

With little curlicues all around my head.

Looking like a lollipop-licking five-year-old.

Or a poodle.

Fortunately Kenzie isn't here today, so I don't have to face her judgmental gaze.

"So, Maya, what's up with your hair?" someone behind me asks. "It's super-cute. What's the special occasion? Boyfriend?" She's a Band Geek, a seven on the Popularity Scale.

"Maya, with a boyfriend? Don't be stupid," her friend whispers.

I think of my beloved crush Ethan who hardly notices me, even with my new outrageous hairstyles. Who am I kidding? This girl is right.

Carlos Sanchez just looks at me, raises his eyebrows, and doesn't say anything.

That itself is criticism enough.

Later I find out that next Friday is picture day! I have to see what Betty Cornell says about how to prepare for such an event. This could end up being a very big factor in my rise to popularity. My hair's going frizzy just thinking about it.

. . . .

Tuesday, October 11

Brodie and I are doing impressions of *ranchera* singers. We swish our hair back and forth to the radio. We even write a song using all the Spanish words we know. It's sung to the tune of "Suddenly Seymour" from the musical *Little Shop of Horrors*.

El Casa Burrito

El Taco y Queso

La Mamá, El Papá

Soy papas con huevos

ROUGH TRANSLATION:

The House of Burrito

Taco and Cheese

Mom, Dad

I am potatoes with eggs (or testicles)

It's obvious my Spanish is lacking.

Mom wanders into my room and lies down next to me. We talk and laugh for a while. I sing her our freshly composed song in Spanish.

"You almost got the *el*'s and *la*'s right." She laughs.

"What do you mean?"

"You know, everything in Spanish is either masculine or feminine. I explained this to Brodie just this morning when we were waiting for his bus."

"You gave my little brother the masculine/feminine talk while *waiting for the bus*?!"

"Yah, we had a spare moment. So I told him about how it all works."

I'm a little horrified. This can't be what I think it is, can it? "We aren't talking about the same masculine/feminine thing, are we? Brodie still thinks girls pee standing up."

Mom realizes what I mean and smacks me with a pillow. I laugh.

"Brodie, get in here!" Brodie comes in, red-faced and embarrassed, obviously aware of what we've been discussing. "Tell me, do girls pee standing up?" I ask.

"I don't think that I should hear this," he mumbles after a few seconds of silence.

Mom shudders. She and Dad have been putting off "The Talk" with Brodie for the past forever. "Look, kiddo," she says after it's clear he's confused. "Guys have outdoor plumbing, girls have indoor. If we tried to pee standing up, it would just dribble down our legs."

I laugh so hard at the expression on Brodie's face that I fall off my bed.

Wednesday, October 12

Brushing is essential for beautiful hair.
Not just lackadaisical brushing, but good
stiff get-in-there-and-dig brushing. . . .
To be adequately brushed, hair should
be stroked at least one hundred times each
night.

After I can no longer feel my arm and my hair is smooth as silk, I curl up under my covers. Dad comes into my bedroom. He kisses me good night and his hair falls all over my face. My dad has been growing out his hair for the last two years. Mom's not crazy about the style, but understands that he's doing it not only for his war re-enacting gig, but also because he wants to fully revel in his hair while he still has it. A last hurrah. He says that his students used to come to him for advice because he was always dressed properly in a tie with hair trimmed short. He seemed like a father figure.

Now, he tells me, they come to admit their wrongdoings. I think it's because, with his hair grown out to his shoulders all curly and his unshaven sympathetic face, he kind of looks like Jesus.

Thursday, October 13

Kenzie and I are walking to our first-period classes. She pauses and takes a long look at me. "Okay, dude, what the hell is up with your hair? Seriously, I mean this is weird, even for you!"

This morning Mom helped me put my hair in two tiny buns on either side of my head. It looks like mushrooms are sprouting out of my skull. "I was going for the Princess Leia look," I mutter.

"Who the hell is that?" Kenzie asks.

I roll my eyes. Kenzie has never watched *Star Wars*. Or eaten applesauce. Or seen *Sesame Street*. A deprived childhood if I've ever seen one.

I walk into algebra and sit down. Anna looks over at me and smiles. "I like your buns, Maya."

The guy next to her lets out a really loud, obnoxious laugh. She goes red and looks down, mortified.

. . . .

By sixth period my hair has started to fall out of the buns, so it looks as if my mushrooms are growing fur. I go into the bathroom to see what I can do about it, but every single sink has three or four girls (all fours on My School's Popularity Scale—Less-Popular Girls Who Dress Seductively) trying to see their reflections. Their jeans look as if they cut off the circulation to their legs, and their glowing red bras (visible beneath their yellow polo shirts) match their thickly applied blush. I wait a few minutes in the vain hope that someone will leave, but when one girl starts curling her eyelashes and plucking her eyebrows, I know that's not going to happen. I head to class, fuzzy fungi and all.

All of our Thirteen Colonies map assignments are on a table outside the door to history. Carlos Sanchez is playing with mine, pretending it's a spaceship.

"Don't touch Maya's project," says one boy.

Carlos Sanchez looks down at me. "This is your project?" he asks. I nod. "It looks delicious," he continues. "I wish that I could get inside it, if you know what I mean." He raises his eyebrows. I assume he thinks he's sexy, but in reality, it makes him look like he has a forehead twitch.

"Do you have the answers (*twitch, twitch*) for the homework?" he asks me.

"I'm not giving you the answers."

"Dumbass," he says, tossing my project down on the table. That seems just a little ironic.

. . . .

Picture day tomorrow! I am so excited!

> One of the most-looked-at pictures any
> teen has taken is the picture for her school
> yearbook. This picture need not ever cause any
> qualms if you give some thought to it. . . . To a
> photography appointment wear a white tailored
> blouse . . . Wear no jewelry, except perhaps a
> strand of pearls.

Mom bought me a pretty white blouse at the thrift store earlier today. But as far as the necklace goes, I don't know where to look. I decide to check out Mom's discarded 1980s jewelry box. She's bound to have something.

Yep. I find the pearls within ten seconds of looking. I've never been forced to view so many pairs of giant, abstract earrings before. I'm a little worried about the horrible mental scars that may afflict me later in life. My personal favorite is a bulky, puce-colored, plastic bracelet that opens with a hinge. Mom got it in Paris. Of all the things to buy in Europe. There are no excuses.

I wash my hair and carefully set out my clothes for tomorrow. Mom helps me put my locks in curlers (looser this time) and even lends me some shiny lip gloss.

I think that tomorrow will be amazing.
At least, that's what I keep telling myself.

~ *Maya's Popularity Tip* ~

Make your yearbook picture memorable because, as my science teacher says, "Your grandkids have to laugh at something."

Friday, October 14

My friend Dante straightened his curly black hair this morning, but apparently it was a catastrophe. So during lunch he sprayed it with water and now it's back to normal. I could have warned him about that.

When taking school pictures, Betty Cornell advises the following: *"Above all, do not change your hairstyle before your appointment—such experiments may turn out too disastrously, and you don't want to go down in history looking like a freak."*

During science, we go to the gym where the photographers are waiting. Most of the boys take their pictures with mug shot–serious expressions and refuse to smile. I wait anxiously, practicing how Betty said to stand: my shoulders twisted slightly, a three-quarter view of my face, keeping in mind that whatever is closest to the camera will appear largest (which is why I try to get my left side closer, because of some lopsidedness in the booby department).

Absently, I turn to Dante and ask him if I look okay.

"To tell you the truth, Maya, you've always reminded me

of a murderer in a horror film. In fact, that's the reason I don't argue with you. I'm afraid you may eat my face off."

Well, that's a fantastic thing to say to a self-conscious girl right before she is about to have her image preserved in the most permanent of ways.

"Van, Van, Wag, Wajen, Vagin, Wogen." A large guy with a handlebar mustache reads off a clipboard.

I step forward, not even bothering to correct him. I'm used to people slaughtering my Dutch surname.

I position my body correctly and give a big smile. I see a flash and my vision goes black.

I hear, "Uh . . . let's try that again . . . Without the glasses."

I swipe the lenses off my face, still dazed. The flash catches me off guard. I'm sure I look hideous.

"I, I wasn't ready. . . ." I stammer, but I'm shuffled over to the side by mustache-guy. I feel defeated and frustrated, but I hold my head high. I'm pretty sure that's what Betty would want me to do.

Monday, October 17

Mom has gotten up early every day to help me change my hair. She's totally awesome. Today she teased it into a really high side ponytail, but not a single person at school has said anything! At church yesterday, Ethan didn't notice my hair, either. But that's not surprising, seeing as how he seldom looks my way. I wonder if I will ever see the day when a boy likes me the same way I like him.

I contemplate this situation while shelving books in the library during lunch. Leon comes in like he does every day, lifting my spirits.

"Hi, Maya."

"Hi, Leon."

"You look beautiful today."

"Thank you."

He goes off to find a book on wolves. Ms. Corbeil catches my eye and motions me over.

"Maya, you know how Leon comes in every day and tells you that you look beautiful?"

I nod.

"I just want to make sure it doesn't make you uncomfortable. I know that because of his autism he says things. You know a lot about autism because of your sister and well . . . if it embarrasses you or makes you uncomfortable, please tell me. I will talk to him about not being so . . . devoted." She smiles sadly. "It's obvious that he has a thing for you. So if he ever says anything inappropriate, let me know."

I stand there looking at her and then at the mirror on the wall. I see a little girl with a side ponytail holding a stack of books close to her. I know Leon has autism. And I'm grateful that Ms. Corbeil is so protective of all of her students in her library. But suddenly I feel my stomach drop.

I walk back to the shelves. Leon looks up at me. "Hi, Maya."

"Hi, Leon," I say.

"You look fabulous," he says. "You look gorgeous. You look beautiful."

"Thanks."

I close my eyes. I realize why it hurts. I was too blind to consider that maybe the only reason he thinks I am beautiful is because of his autism.

Wednesday, October 19

During after-school choir practice all of the Volleyball Girls are crying. They're normally perfect hair looks disheveled and their makeup is smudged. The teacher announces that Julina, one of their own, was called home during eighth period because her dad had died suddenly of a heart attack.

"I can't believe he's dead," one sobs.

"He was like my dad," whispers the girl who's crying the hardest. "He was one of my favorite people."

I stand there, feeling out of place. Without doing anything, Julina has a new identity. She is the girl with the dead father. I understand because much of my life I've been the girl with the dead sister. Ariana died when I was six, on the ninety-ninth day of her life.

Two-year-old Brodie and I stayed at our neighbor's house while Mom and Dad rushed Ariana to the hospital. I swear I knew the exact moment when her damaged heart stopped beating. I was jumping on their trampoline when in midair, time froze. I could feel it. She was gone. That was the moment I went from being a bold, confident first grader to the anxious and fearful introvert that I am today.

At school as everyone whispers and sobs around me, I wonder how this moment will define Julina.

Brodie, Ariana, and me

Thursday, October 27

In the spirit of the Halloween season, I feel it appropriate to share some very odd observations about my neighborhood:

- We can see the smoke from Matamoros, Mexico, as it burns in the drug war.
- I'm pretty sure our neighbor buried a body in his front yard. He's always watering the same patch of green lawn.
- My little brother has a groupie next door. She follows him from the bus and stands outside our house, even when no one's home. The kid's only five years old.
- I suspect there's a drug dealer also; there are way

too many expensive cars and late-night visitors.
For my own safety I dare not say who or where.

- There are dogs that bark all night long. Except
  during earsplitting *ranchera* karaoke parties. It's
  a lose–lose situation.
- A week ago, I saw a life-size nutcracker in our
  neighbor's garage. I still have nightmares.
- Spandex. A lot of Spandex.
- "Speed bumps" here are known as "humps."
  Our house is right behind a "hump" sign.
- Every night a loud burst of static-filled music
  is heard. But there's no need to be alarmed
  because it's just the corn-in-a-cup man trying to
  sell you something to eat.
- A free-roaming chicken wanders the streets all
  day. I've named him Little Sandoval.

Friday, October 28

"So, you're really doing this?" I ask Mom from my perch on
her bathroom sink. She's just put on an oversized T-shirt that
she got way back in her previous life (before kids) when she
and Dad were dirt-poor documentary filmmakers who trav-
eled the world. She brushes out her graying hair so that it
hangs around her shoulders.

"Oh yeah." She speaks with confidence, but I notice how
her voice shakes just a little bit. She's never dyed her hair before. But it's Halloween, so if it goes badly (bleached or bald),
she can simply make it part of a costume. "Thousands of

women dye their hair," she says for the third time in fifteen minutes. "It can't be too bad." She takes a deep breath and reads aloud, "**CAUTION: DO NOT USE THIS PRODUCT TO COLOR EYELASHES OR EYEBROWS. WILL CAUSE BLINDNESS.**"

Yikes.

Thirty minutes later Mom is looking at herself in the foggy mirror.

"Uh-oh," she says. "I think I dyed my ears."

"That's just fantastic," I say.

She plays with different hairstyles, obviously pleased. She digs around in one of the drawers until she finds a stubby brown makeup pencil. "I'm going to be Frida Kahlo for Halloween," she says, drawing a unibrow on her forehead.

"What about the mustache, Mom? Frida Kahlo had a mustache."

"You're right." she laughs, sketching hairs on her upper lip.

"AHHH! You look like a MAN! This is so wrong!" I yell. "Make it stop!"

She chuckles in a deep voice.

I bury my face in my hands.

I hear the sound of the front door opening. Dad calls a cheerful hello, and right away, I can tell he's up to something. He clomps up the stairs and appears in the bathroom with a wicked smile on his face.

His hair is tied back behind his head.

Mom has facial hair like a dude, and Dad has a ponytail like a chick.

Dad stares at Mom, and she looks back at him. They run to each other and kiss. I flee the room. It's all so disorienting. There are just some things you shouldn't see your parents do.

Monday, October 31

For Halloween this year I'm going to be Betty. Not Betty Cornell, but a very different, yet also influential, Betty. Betty Suarez, aka "Ugly Betty," is a brilliant, confident, braces-wearing Latina, with a unique style and powerful sense of self. Mom and I watched all four seasons of the show together over the summer. We're big fans.

We found a frilly purple blouse, a pink flowered skirt, hideous crocodile-print flats, green butterfly socks, and some red-rimmed glasses at the thrift store. At my last orthodontist appointment I even changed the rubber bands on my braces to blue. Brodie is going as Harry Potter, dressed in Mom's old graduation gown. He smiles, showing off his dimples. His light brown hair is almost as long as Dad's, but more California surfer dude. Goodness gracious, he's adorable.

By Brownsville standards, we live in a nice subdivision, so it's a good place to go trick-or-treating. Our neighbors consist of full-time nurses, teachers, FBI agents, suspected drug dealers (as previously mentioned), and at least one registered sex offender (inspiring the relocation of our bus stop). Tonight should be interesting.

It's quickly getting dark as Brodie and I trick-or-treat. He holds my hand as we walk up to the next house. I catch a glimpse of myself in a car window. It looks like my head is being swallowed by an ugly brown alley cat. I ratted and teased my hair out for my costume. I suppose it's fitting that my coifed curtain call is the largest configuration yet.

Overall, the evening turns out rather well. Brodie and I collect loads of candy and see some of his friends decked out in pink curly wigs. I even get leered at by some incredibly drunk neighbors. That's never happened to me before. I guess being noticed is the first step to becoming popular, even if it's by inebriates.

"One of the most important things for any teen to realize is that she is always on display," says Betty Cornell. I may have to watch myself though. If I keep following in her footsteps, maybe someday I'll become so popular that everyone, sober or not, will have to stop and stare. But for now, I'm moving on to bigger and Betty-er things!

My family's Halloween

November

MODELING TRICKS

....

To look your best, you must get in the habit of
standing tall . . . Someone once told me to stand
as if I wore a beautiful jewel that I wanted to
show off at my bosom, and I think perhaps it is
the best advice I can pass on to you.

I read this out loud to Mom, Betty Cornell's book in my hands.
She smiles, stirring leftover chili at the stove.

Brodie looks up from his homework. "What's a bosom?"

Indeed, what is a bosom? I probably will never know.

In this next chapter called "Modeling Tricks," Betty recommends that I sit and stand tall with shoulders back. I should
walk with fluid leg movements and boobs thrust forward to

greet the world (okay, those last words are mine. If she'd uttered "boobs" back in the 1950s she probably would've been burned at the stake).

When I was four years old I started ballet and continued until I was nine. During those years I was most aware of how I carried my body. Still, I never belonged with any of the tall willowy blond girls who looked as if they'd been spun from sugar and would break if touched. I was built more like a brick. Heavy and sturdy. Mom finally let me quit after my kneecap dislocated.

So, at one time I was good at sitting up straight and tiptoeing along. Now . . . not so much. So, all I've got to do is reconnect with my inner ballerina.

Practicing posture

Wednesday, November 2

You never see a model slouch, you never see a model with her fanny poked out or her chin resting on her breastbone. A model knows that good posture is basic to a good figure, and that a good carriage goes hand in hand with good posture.

I walk lightly down to the bus stop, sucking in my stomach. I pull myself up into one straight line, even though it hurts my shoulders. Later, in history class, I keep up my good posture. It's definitely a challenge. Mr. Santiago keeps the room so cold that it forces me to go into hibernation mode. All we do the entire period today is read out of the textbook. He has a talent for making influential breakthroughs and conflicts as boring as counting tiles on the ceiling. I try to stay awake by doodling Ethan's name in the margins of my notebook.

All of a sudden I hear some girls screaming at each other in Spanish. The commotion seems to come from the hall. I look up from my scribbling. More screaming. Mr. Santiago closes the door and goes on with his lesson.

Later, I find out that the yelling was from two pregnant girls who got in a rather heated fight. There was a lot of name calling and hair pulling, but security personnel intervened before they could do any real damage to each other.

. . . .

Thursday, November 3

Thanks to an ill-fitting bra, I grab my PE clothes and change my shirt in the bathroom stalls. The Volleyball Girls watch me as I go, their faces annoyingly blank. I wish Kenzie was here, but she's sick today.

As I walk into the gym I feel everyone's eyes turn toward me, but not in the Cinderella-arrives-at-the-ball way. It feels more like the pigeon-walks-into-a-room-full-of-peacocks way.

Then I realize I am the only one dressed in ugly PE clothes. I panic.

Finally, I force myself to take a deep breath and try to imagine what Betty Cornell would do.

So I smile, showing my electric blue braces, shove my shoulders back, and draw myself up to my full height.

"Hey, look guys," says Carlos Sanchez, "she's trying to be a model!"

Maybe I am.

Monday, November 7

We're almost a third of the way through the school year. I don't feel popular, but I still change up my hair once a week just to keep people guessing. Today, I make my way to algebra concentrating on my legs, imagining Ethan is watching. Betty Cornell explains the best way to stroll like a model.

> *To walk gracefully one must move the leg in one piece. . . . In that way, the leg moves forward in*

one sweeping movement, instead of propelling
itself by a series of awkward disjointed jerks.

This is actually harder than it sounds in a hallway full of screaming kids all pushing and shoving. Around me everyone is talking:

"He's such a lying, dirty, perverted scumbag! I can't believe I actually..."

"Did you see the thing in the girl's bathroom? It looked like pot."

"Like I told you, Sophie, the French are idiots."

"I heard somewhere that a dork is what's between a whale's legs."

Suddenly someone crashes into me, and my backpack strap snaps. It's now hanging off my left shoulder. No! I have to lean over, slouching with my right arm bent around my back to keep my stuff from falling out.

Forget posture—I limp along trying to maintain my dignity.

. . . .

When Mom picks me up from school, I tell her that I went to see one of Mr. Lawrence's friends (my old history teacher) to ask why Mr. Lawrence has been absent for so long.

"He said Mr. Lawrence is very sick," I say, looking down at the ground. "If he comes back it won't be until after Christmas. That's all the information I could get out of him."

I'm starting to wonder now if Mr. Lawrence will come back at all.

. . . .

I'm reading my Betty Cornell book on my bed. I open the front cover and notice an inscription in careful cursive.

To Le Nore,
From Mama and Daddy
1953

I wonder how old Le Nore was when she held this same book in her hands. What did she look like? Did she ask for it, or was it thrown at her by observant parents who felt bad when they saw that their little girl had no friends? Did the book help her, or did it sit on a shelf for nearly forty years before being dropped off at a donation center?

I wish this book could talk. I bury my nose in its faded words and yellowing pages and breathe in the smell. I've always loved to read. Mom and Dad made sure that I brought a book with me wherever I went, the way some parents would insist you bring a jacket.

When I was seven, they gave me a copy of *Old Yeller.* Eager to hear the happy story of a boy and his dog, I began reading it immediately. Halfway through, in the middle of the night, I realized what would happen to poor Old Yeller. I became an inconsolable, sobbing mess and ran to the basement where Dad was working. I told him that I couldn't take it. He held me for a long time while I cried, and then told me that the author had forgotten to include a chapter at the end of the book. He sat for an hour with me on his lap and wrote the "final" section to the novel. It described how Old Yeller didn't really die, that it was a different dog that looked like him but was evil because he ate kittens. Old Yeller lived happily ever after in a just world that (I'd already learned with the death of my sister) was light-years away from reality. That chapter is still taped in the back cover of *Old Yeller*, and every time I read it I smile.

Tuesday, November 8

"This is an official lockdown. Please go to your lockdown areas in a calm and orderly fashion."

We all jump at the sound of the principal on the speaker. I put my choir binder down on one of the risers and turn to Anita, the girl who's standing next to me. She seems a little annoyed.

In Brownsville, so close to the Mexican border, we have "lockdown drills" more often than we do fire drills.

At the border wall

For the last few years a violent drug war has raged between Mexican drug cartels and the Mexican military, leaving tens of thousands dead and missing. Terrible things have spilled over our border: drugs, shootings, kidnappings. Last year our school was on lockdown one afternoon because of a secret FBI drug operation going on down the street. There were even helicopters flying over and agents in our parking lot. Dad was furious when I told him about it and personally complained to the local director of the FBI. He said it was absolutely insane for them to do something like that during school hours.

Cartel battle in Mexico as viewed from Dad's office

So, as the principal announces this lockdown, I think through the familiar procedure: lock the doors, hide in the classroom, and turn off the lights. Then, all of a sudden a panicked woman's voice booms through the intercom.

"MANDATORY LOCKDOWN! NOW! NOW! NOW!"

I know right away that this isn't just a drill. Anita bursts into frightened sobs. I grab her hand. Forget about orderly fashion; we run. We hide in a storage closet in the band room. There are twenty girls in all. Ms. Fletcher, our assistant choir director comes in, her voice quiet, but stern.

"Don't say anything," she whispers.

The room is dead silent. No one breathes. When a room full of middle school girls is so quiet that you can hear a pin drop, something is very wrong.

We hear thumps in the distance. Anita lets out a whimper.

All I can think of is my family. Natalia, Dad, Mom, Brodie. I curl up into a fetal position. The worst thing is the silence. The dark. The fact that I have no idea what's happening. The fact that not even the teachers, the adults in charge, know what's going on.

We sit for what feels like hours when sirens blare.

Ms. Fletcher peeks through the window.

"Don't say anything, girls, please stay quiet. Don't make any noise. Don't talk."

Tears begin to cloud my vision. I fold up, hugging my knees close to me.

What does it feel like to die? Will I ever see sunshine again? Will I ever get to tell my family how much I love them?

"Please, don't move. . . ." Ms. Fletcher murmurs. Her voice is hardly a whisper.

We sit for over an hour, trembling and crying. Then suddenly, the lights go back on. We slowly walk back to our class, dazed by the fluorescent white. We sit back on the risers and learn about how to build a five chord.

"So you see how the notes can be switched around . . ."

Just like it never happened.

It wouldn't be until we watched the news tonight that we learned the police were chasing an armed robbery suspect through the neighborhood directly across the street from our school. What kind of world do we live in?

Wednesday, November 9

Today Natalia is officially six. The living room is scattered with wrapping paper and string, and Natalia carries around a toy horse in each hand looking like she just might fall over with excitement. It's always so cool to see the way she smiles when she opens a *Wonder Pets* DVD.

"How old are you, Natalia?" Dad leans down and kisses her forehead.

"Four," she says, in the same way that we taught her two years ago. When some things get drilled into her head, they're stuck for good.

"No, you're six."

"Sex..."

"How old are you?"

"Four." She smiles at us, showing her pointy teeth. I still have the scar on my chest where she bit through my dress three years ago. I'd grabbed her to keep her from running into the street.

"No, Natalia, you're six."

"Four!" She's frustrated now. *"Madre Santa!"* she shouts.

I love it when my little sister swears in Spanish.

. . . .

Friday, November 11

Many teens seem to walk head first into
everything—that is to say, they lead with
their chin. This aggressive attitude comes
from standing with the head jutted forward,
shoulders slumped, and eyes focused on the
ground.

This definitely sums up the posture at my school.

I walk (Betty Cornell style) into my science class and see that Ms. Cordova is ready to lecture. I pull out a pencil from my "sling" (which once served as a backpack), and I straighten my spine and stand up as tall as I can. My vertebrae pop and I wince.

All of a sudden, Carlos Sanchez and his buddy Pablo come running in from the hall. Pablo snatches the pencil from my desk, and the two of them begin an epic sword fight behind Ms. Cordova's back. They spring to and fro, dancing around, attacking each other with the sharpened points. The class cheers them on. I realize that Pablo isn't going to give back my stolen property, so I march up to him, head high. I nimbly grab the pencil from his hand just as he's about to make a brave thrust at Carlos Sanchez.

Then, I remember my manners. I look him in the eyes. "Thank you," I say, and walk back to my seat.

One of the worst faults most of us have is that we
do not stand up. Even when we are in a vertical
position in relation to the ground, we still tend
to sit down. Our rib cages are slumped into our

waistline and our shoulders are bent forward.
One way to correct this habit is to concentrate on
your rib cage.

Some of the other kids begin to stare at me. Slowly, as if intimidated, they sit up straighter and glare at me for making them feel slouchy.

Three cheers for positive peer pressure.

Monday, November 14

"Guess what, Maya." Kenzie is flushed with excitement. "I got a *boyfriend!*"

"What?"

"Yep," she beams.

"Who?" I ask.

"Angel. We were in PE with him in sixth grade."

"I remember. The slouchy one." Betty would not approve of Angel's posture. "Is he nice?" I ask, thinking of my (generally sweet) nerdy crushes. Ethan is both kind and intelligent.

"He's got a *mustache.*"

I bite my lip. Come on, *be a good friend.* "Okay," I say. "Just, don't let him do anything to you, all right? You deserve so much better than that."

"Never," she promises.

The bus comes to a stop and I stand up. She gives me a quick hug. I force a smile, but I'm not sure how long I can handle this new, bubbly, affectionate Kenzie.

. . . .

Tuesday, November 15

Today I take the leap. Today I put away the pads. Today I join the legions of tampon-wearing women all over the developed world.

In Brownsville tampons are seen as immoral. So is using birth control. What I don't understand is that teen pregnancy is generally accepted.

It's kind of scary using tampons for the first time, but Mom has always been very open with her information. She tells me everything that she had to find out by herself, because her family didn't talk about these kinds of things.

"When using a pad, place it in the middle," she'd told me when I started using them. "And for goodness sakes, put the adhesive side *down.*"

"Don't ever flush pads down the toilet."

"And I can't stress this enough: after you put a tampon in, *take the applicator out!*"

Growing up listening to horror stories can really mess with your head, but it's better to know than to have to learn the hard way.

Poor Mom.

Wednesday, November 16

At church, I sit with my friend Liliana, with whom I've been close since we moved to Brownsville a little over two years ago. She was my first best friend, before Kenzie. She is the kind of person who works so hard to do the right thing, will watch out for you, and keep you company if you're feeling lonely. Since we don't go to the same school, we'd spend as much time as we could together at church, laughing and swapping secrets. But we've drifted apart as so many friends do. This doesn't stop me from wanting to be near her, though.

We sit together and sort through canned goods for a food drive. Ethan, my dashing, darling crush, walks over. My heart almost stops.

He smiles at Liliana.

He laughs and makes jokes—for her.

I try to tell him about my school, but it comes out like nonsense. I make a joke, and he doesn't laugh. Liliana says the same thing, and he's practically rolling on the ground.

I sit staring at the floor. It doesn't take a genius to figure out what's happening.

At first all I feel is numbness. Then hurt. Loads and loads of hurt.

"What's wrong?" Mom asks when I get in the car.

"I think Ethan likes Liliana."

She winces and nods. We're silent until we get home. Dad is sitting in the living room. "Maya's having boy troubles," she blurts. I shoot her a warning look and she gets quiet.

"It's no big deal. He's a thirteen-year-old boy." I try to make it seem like it's nothing, but make an excuse to run to my room as soon as I can.

A few minutes later Dad comes upstairs and sits on the side of my bed. He tries to make me feel better by telling me "when-I-was-a-kid" stories. I keep my voice light and laugh at all his jokes. I can see that he's relieved so I kiss him good night.

But when he walks out the door, I cry myself to sleep. The word crush is not ironic. It's the truth.

Thursday, November 17

I do my best to hold my head high as I walk to the bus stop. (*"It may seem like a little thing, but an ungainly walk can be the ruin of even the most attractive girl,"* says Betty). Since I am definitely not the most attractive, I guess I'll just have to work extra hard on my posture. I don't have much else going for me. It turns out I'm not the only one having love problems.

"Mornin'," I say to Kenzie as I sit behind her.

She raises her eyebrows and looks up from her paranormal romance novel. "Okay."

"So, how's your new boyfriend?"

She snaps her raspberry gum, "We broke up yesterday."

"Oh." I make a sympathetic face, but actually I'm relieved. I missed the old Kenzie.

"He wants me back, though."

"He has a mustache."

"I *know!* What the hell was I thinking going out with him?"

We giggle for a while then get down to our usual discussion about whether or not swear words from the Bible can be used in school assignments. It's fantastic to have her back again.

. . . .

It's the A-Honor-Roll Party during ninth period. It sounds cool because we get to miss class, but it's just a bunch of nerds who sit around and eat junk food. I pick up a slice of pizza and walk around the room for a little while, unsure of where to sit, reminded yet again that I don't belong anywhere.

"Yo, Maya, you can sit with us if you really want to," a choir girl says. Surprised, I join her group. I don't understand their inside jokes or know the people they are referring to, so I sit quietly and stare down at my plate.

Out of the corner of my eye, I see another girl, alone. Everyone else nearby has scooted away, leaving her with nearly half an empty table. She doesn't seem to mind though, and eats quietly.

I want to sit with her.

Suddenly, my heart won't be still. Will I offend the girls I'm with by walking away to sit with someone who's obviously ranked lower than them on the Popularity Scale?

I take a deep breath.

A deep breath will show you how much you can bring your whole chest area up into the air.

Not what I meant, Betty.

I walk over to her. "Hi there!" I say before I can talk myself out of it. "What's your name?" The words ring with a confidence that surprises me.

She looks up. "Donna," she says, as if she's unsure.

"It's nice to meet you, Donna." I smile, waiting for her to ask my name, but she seems kind of shocked. I sit down across from her. "What grade are you in this year?"

"Sixth."

"That's cool, how do you like it so far?" I continue. "It's quite a change from elementary to middle school. But you seem to be coping with it well."

"Okay."

"So what's your favorite subject, Donna?"

She doesn't pause to think. "English. I love to write."

"No way, that's my favorite subject! I love writing, too!"

Her eyes light up as she tells me about her favorite author and recent short stories she's written. The bell rings and she and I get up.

"What's your name?" she finally asks, looking up at me.

"Maya," I say.

She repeats it as if she wants to remember it.

"It was really cool meeting you, Donna," I say. "See you later!"

I leave for choir practice and watch her disappear in the opposite direction. I think I see her smile.

Monday, November 28

It's Monday and it's back to the early-morning routine. I'm

forced to wake up, brush my hair, and correct my posture (which has actually gotten pretty good). When we get to school, Kenzie and I head to the library.

"Hey, Maya. Why are you walking funny?"

"I'm not walking funny."

"Yes, you are."

"This is how people should walk."

"No . . ." A look of realization dawns on her face. "I get it! You're trying to make your boobs look bigger!"

"Am not!"

She does a quick imitation of me with boobs thrust forward and laughs. "Bigger boobs, bigger boobs."

I sigh. This is what having good posture can do to you.

Tuesday, November 29

Apparently Mom tried to have "The Talk" with Brodie today. He was really upset by something he heard at school, so rather than wait until Dad came home, she took the lead. This rare rite of passage is usually reserved for father/son camping trips, but Dad's hardly ever home these days. He works crazy hours in his office to finish his next book and hopefully open an escape hatch for our family, one that will get us away from FBI drug busts in the school parking lot.

Mom: Do you have any questions about anything?

Brodie: Am I in trouble?

Mom: No, it's just that I want to talk to you about life and stuff . . .

Brodie: (plugging ears) I don't want to know! I don't want

to know! (Bolts from the couch and hides in the bathroom)

Maybe we should just drop the boy off at a farm for a week or two. He'll learn everything he needs to know.

Wednesday, November 30

Natalia has a horseback riding lesson today. She's had a few and loves them, despite the fact that when we point to a horse she says, "Cow. Moo." I decide to tag along.

As we drive out to the ranch, I think over this past month and Betty Cornell's modeling tips. Here's the summation of my findings:

- Nobody at school cares about posture.
- I got very few comments about my walk (other than from Kenzie and Carlos Sanchez).
- I don't feel any more popular this month.
- Therefore, maybe sitting up straight doesn't really matter?

Mom pulls into the gate and I unbuckle Natalia, who's bursting with excitement. She's flapping her hands so hard I'm afraid she might take flight. She smiles her biggest and asks, "Ride? Ride?"

I hug her and she runs in her rose-colored cowboy boots to the stable where she goes to brush the horse, Simon, before putting on her pink helmet. Simon is the color of old socks that have been washed several thousand times. He drools, has no teeth, but he's gentle with Nat, and that's what matters.

Natalia and Simon

Mom and the trainer, Miss Stacy, help Natalia lead the horse into the enclosed riding area. I sit outside on one of the rusted lawn chairs and think sad thoughts. I can't believe this posture thing has amounted to nothing. I'm so distracted that I almost don't hear the conversation going on next to me.

Miss Stacy is telling Mom about the horse shows where her students compete.

"You know, the reason that kids don't win," she says, "is because they're lazy."

"How so?" Mom asks.

"They slouch. I'm constantly telling them that they have

to sit up straight to win, but they don't listen." She watches my little sister circle around the ring. "Natalia has a fantastic stance."

She's right. Natalia always stands tall. I watch as she raises her arms and squeals with joy. She sits straight, head held high, showing the world how fantastic she is.

"Posture is everything," I hear Miss Stacy say.

I smile, and in spite of my dreary attitude, I draw myself up, tummy tucked in, and show off my bosom.

Keep your muscles in trim and your body in line
so you need never fear how you look.

Maybe posture isn't such a waste of time after all.

December

SKIN PROBLEMS & MAKEUP

· ·

No teenager is ever stuck with the face she was
born with, in view of the ways she has to make up
her features to their best advantage . . .

I've only worn makeup in plays or ballet recitals, but dragonfly
and flower costumes don't really give you a feel for how the
world of "big girl" makeup works. Of course I've experi-
mented. When I was six my aunt bought me a whole set
of makeup that included orange and purple lipsticks and
mountains of glitter. But every time I wore it I'd end up
looking like the prostitutes who hang out on 14th Street in
downtown Brownsville.

Mom, who is naturally gorgeous, rarely wears makeup.

Once a year, she goes all out for a wedding or some other special occasion. But other than that—nothing.

So you can understand why I'm sweating as I stand with Mom in the grocery store makeup aisle, leaning over a **MATCH YOUR SKIN TONE** poster, trying to figure out what color powder matches my undertones.

"There's no way you're porcelain," my brown-skinned mother says, holding my hand under the plastic guide. "There are a lot of people lighter than you."

"That's what it says."

"Well, I guess we'll just have to get it then," she concedes, tossing it into the grocery cart. "What else do we need?"

I think back to Betty Cornell's list:

- Powder
- Mild face lotion that serves as a powder base
- Lipstick (*"clear reds and strong pinks are good colors to work with"*)
- Lipstick brush
- Nail polish that harmonizes with lipstick
- Nail base
- Clear nail polish
- Emery board
- Skin cleanser
- Cotton powder puffs
- Cuticle stick

My head is swirling with information.

I recite the list to Mom who finds a tube of red lipstick. "Are you sure you don't need rouge?"

"Betty Cornell says that I don't."

Few teen-agers need to add color, for their skins have a glowing light of their own derived from an active outdoor life.

I'm counting on PE to provide this.

After we finish shopping, Mom and I get into the car. She looks at me really hard and smiles. "Wow, Maya. You are seriously ballsy."

"Thanks . . . I guess."

"I mean it. When I was in middle school, I never would've dreamed of doing a fraction of what you're willing to do."

I smile. Growing up, I was the quiet girl who no one talked to. I was the one who would blend in until the teacher called on me. And if I volunteered answers too often, the class would go silent, drawing an even larger barrier between us.

And now, look at me. I'm sitting in a minivan with new makeup on my lap, trying to earn the approval, the trust, and the admiration of those who I'd gone out of my way to avoid all my life.

Saturday, December 3

"Come on out, Maya, show us your makeup!" Dad's voice drifts in from the living room, where he sits waiting with the rest of the family.

"No."

"Come on! We haven't got all day!"

They have to get bored sometime. Maybe if I just stay in the bathroom with the door locked they'll forget about me.

"Hurry!" Brodie shouts.

I hear Mom walk to the door. "Maya, it's okay. Come on out."

"I look like a clown-whore." I whimper.

Even through the wood, I hear her stifle a laugh. "I'm sure you don't look like a clown-whore, baby."

I look in the mirror and shudder. I followed Betty Cornell's advice exactly. How did it go so wrong?

Finally, I unlock the door and walk outside.

Mom looks at me. She bites her lip. My cheeks go red, but she probably can't tell.

"Honey, you have powder streaks all over your face. The goal is for it to be subtle."

"Oh."

She helps me fix it and pushes me into the living room to show the rest of the family. Brodie looks up at me and whistles before proceeding to make pigeon noises in Natalia's face. Dad smiles. "You look very nice." He's just saying that because he feels obligated to. Or Mom is behind me whispering threats.

Kenzie will think I've gone nuts!

. . . .

Monday, December 5

I wake up this morning a dithering, sweaty mess. My hand shakes as I apply my new red lipstick (with a new lipstick brush so that I can shape my mouth into *"the most enticing one possible."* Soon, I force myself out the door. The red and yellow lights of the school bus pull around the corner. When the door screeches open, my heart stops. Slowly I climb the steps to my doom.

Keeping my face down, I sit behind Kenzie. It's rather dark outside, so after a while I think she just doesn't notice. Then her forehead wrinkles.

"Are you wearing . . . lip . . . stick?" Her voice is dangerously calm.

"Um, yeah?"

"Why?"

"Uh," I stammer. Finally, I think of a response. "It's for fun!"

She watches me carefully. "Are you wearing . . . *eye shadow*?" On the last word, her voice comes out as a high-pitched shriek.

I look around nervously, but no one's paying attention. Everyone on the bus is either passed out or on their phones. Betty Cornell makes it very clear that we shouldn't use eye makeup at our young age:

> *As to making up your eyes, don't. Young eyes need no enhancement. They have their own sparkle and flashes of fire, so why bury them under gobs of goo? Mascara and eyebrow pencil . . . are artifices best left to others. Teen-*

agers who come to school with colored blobs above each eyelid look plain silly. If you are going somewhere extra special . . . and you feel that you just have to look glamorous, then try a little Vaseline or cream on each eyelid. Just this little touch will bring out all you need to give your eyes a triumphant twinkle.

"Actually, it's Vaseline." I smile innocently, even though my heart is pounding out of my chest. I giggle nervously.

Kenzie's lip begins to twitch . . . literally. "So, you're wearing Vaseline . . . on your eyelids." It's not a question. She's just working through it.

She stares at me for a long time and finally just shakes her head. "You're cute," she says, and turns around.

From the way she glowers, I can tell it's not a compliment.

Tuesday, December 6

I have zits. Quite a few of them. It's not a medical condition like that poor girl in my science class (her name changed from Diane Acbey to Diane Acne overnight), but I still have tons of clogged pores.

Betty Cornell says washing my face is the best thing to do for zits. I have some super-fancy facial soap, but it doesn't really work unless I use it, which I often forget to do. I'll have to be better this month. I mean seriously, I spent the entire summer with a fiery red zit in the middle of my forehead. It looked like a bindi.

Betty Cornell says that I should wash my face with hot water to open my pores and then scrub it with soap, applying it in upward strokes (because *"pulling down on the facial tissues will, after a period of time, tend to make the muscles go slack"*). Then, I rinse with cold water. Twice a week I'm supposed to use ice cubes to fully close my pores.

Betty Cornell doesn't use the word zit, though. She calls them "hickies." This makes me chuckle every time I read it, because I doubt that modern "hickies" and 1950s "hickies" are the same thing. If they were, it could put a whole new spin on this chapter.

. . . .

"Are you still wearing your jelly?" Kenzie inquires in front of our PE locker. "You know . . . *petroleum* jelly."

"Yep."

"You're insane," she says. It's true. Did you know that when you wear Vaseline on your eyelids, it smears onto your glasses and then melts so that it covers the entire lens? Try it sometime.

I pull off my pants and I hear a snarl of disgust behind me. I turn around to see Flor, the leader of the Goth Art Chicks, glaring at me. "Maya!" she yells. "Every time I turn my head I see your giant ass in my face! I don't know what the hell you think it looks like, but it's not pretty! So MOVE!"

She shoves past me to change on a different side of the

room. Tears sting my eyes. But I steady myself and pull on my shorts.

> ~ *Maya's Popularity Tip* ~
> Never cry at school. Ever. Especially
> when it could smudge your Vaseline.

Friday, December 9

How do models deal with fading lipstick? Mine seems to disappear within ten minutes. Betty Cornell says to use a little powder on the lips before applying it and then blot any extra with a tissue. But that doesn't work very well. Maybe it's because I wear cheap grocery store makeup.

I spend two hours on a teen fashion website searching for answers. After taking seven or eight quizzes, I find out the following:

- My skin is "super oily"
- My "fave look" is "natural"
- My "winter hairstyle" is "upswept bun"
- My "celeb skin match" is Selena Gomez
- My eye makeup should be "Sexy and Chic"
  (Like that's going to happen!)

It is horrifying to realize how much time I'd wasted on the website. Normally I prefer reading classic works of literature. I don't know what kept me looking at the stories and articles for so long. I guess it was kind of like that time my cousin and I looked at gossip magazines for an afternoon. It was more like a guilty fixation with something so otherworldly and unachievable.

Sunday, December 11

I wear makeup to church today. Every time I see Ethan, it hurts. As he passes, Dad grabs my wrist.

"What are you doing?" I ask, angry.

"Your pulse sped up when he walked by. You still like him." He smiles, obviously thinking that he's being clever. He's not.

"It sped up because I was nervous because you grabbed me," I babble. I lower my voice. "I don't like him anymore, so leave me alone."

"So who do you like? Dante?"

"No one, okay?"

He raises his eyebrows. "You can't just not like anyone. When I was your age I had crushes on at least five girls at a time. And not one of them liked me back."

He doesn't understand what I feel. Whenever I have a crush on someone, it can last years, and it's always just for one person.

The day I realized I had a crush on Ethan was when some of the girls at church locked me in a closet for the first time. They were mean. They tried to turn others against me, painted all over me at slumber parties, and lied about me to adults.

As I sat huddled in the corner of the dark closet, I heard

Ethan telling off the girls for being awful to me. He shouted, "Go away. Leave her alone!" and he unlocked the door.

Then he smiled at me. My heart melted and my head turned to jelly, petroleum jelly. I knew that I liked him. A lot. Ever since that day he stood up for me, I've liked him. A lot. And as much as I try to convince Dad, Mom, and myself of the opposite, I still like him.

A lot.

Monday, December 12

"Come on, Brodie, I need you!" I shout down the stairs to my little brother.

"What do you want?!" he screams back.

"Come here and I'll tell you!"

"FINE!"

He makes his way upstairs stomping his feet on every step.

"Can you help me do my fingernails?" I ask in my sweetest voice.

"No way!" He pretends to gag himself and heads back toward the stairs.

"If you do, you get to watch TV. I won't tell Mom."

He freezes. Then he turns and comes back to help me.

When your nails are filed and the cuticles softened, you are ready to put on the nail base ... Cover the whole nail with the base and let it dry thoroughly before you start the polish. After the base has dried,

the next step is to apply the first coat of polish.
Cover the whole nail; it is easier than trying to
describe an accurate curve around the moon.

Ten seconds later I'm explaining Betty Cornell's nail regime, telling him I've already filed them into shape and applied a base coat. But I make a mess with the color and gloss layers and need some help. He nods sympathetically and begins applying the polish.

"Are you surprised that I'm doing so good?" he asks after a few minutes.

"Yep, you're amazing."

"I don't like makeup, but I'm still really good."

I was there when Mom got the ultrasound confirming that Brodie was a boy. I wigged. Hard. The only thing I wanted was an older sister or a puppy. The last thing I expected was a little brother. In fact, I didn't even think it was possible and was convinced my parents were doing it just to spite me. So when Brodie was two or three years old, I dressed him up in my clothes and put all sorts of "pretty" stuff on him (thanks to my aunt's gift of sparkly makeup). He's had an irrational fear of lipstick or anything "girly" ever since.

"Maybe you can pay me," he says, finishing the right hand and moving on to the left.

"Uhhh . . ."

"Oh, not a lot, you know, just a shiny penny."

I agree. He does his best, but it turns out quite lumpy and goopy.

"Wow, I'm doing super good. And I just learned!"

"A regular professional," I say, trying to make him feel good.

He's silent for a while, and he finishes the red and goes on to the gloss. He's very proud of how it looks. It makes me smile.

"Okay," he says, as if asking me to listen up. "The key to a perfect nail job is making it look lush. The more color you do, the more lusher it is."

"That's nice."

"So . . . how much *are* you going to pay me?"

Friday, December 16

It's the last day of school before Christmas vacation, and I've applied a special coat of red lipstick. Kenzie and I sit next to each other on the bus ride home. She's going to London over break to see her cousin. The perks of being the only child of gainfully employed parents, I guess.

"I'm so sad though, because I'm going to freeze my butt off," she whines.

"Oh you poor baby. My heart *weeps* for you," I say. "You're going to LONDON! You don't get pity."

She smiles. "And Paris. So did anything interesting happen today?"

I nod. "Carlos Sanchez has become the new teacher's pet in our reading class, because he was the first to answer a question about metaphors. The teacher told us that we 'should all be more like Carlos Sanchez!' I'm not kidding. It really happened!"

I sigh, "I'm so mad! You don't come back till the Thursday after school starts again! I'm going to miss you, Kenzie."

"You too, Lipstick Girl," she says through a mouthful of cupcake she stole from the sixth grader behind us. It turns her teeth red. She wipes some frosting on my shoulder, so I wipe it back on her. The bus pulls up to my stop.

"Bye!" I shout as I get off and watch my best friend through the window.

She waves. *Bye, Maya,* she mouths.

Sunday, December 18

Piano recital tonight. And since Ethan and I have the same teacher, he's going to be there too. As much as I hate myself for it, I still take extra time to make sure that my makeup is nice. Putting on lipstick and powder has become almost second nature to me now. I don't even think twice about it in the mornings anymore. It's very interesting how I've changed.

I wear a red sweater, black slacks, and flats. Dad looks at me funny and raises his eyebrows, knowing that Ethan is going. I ignore him.

We have our recital at a little Unitarian Church downtown. It's very pretty, but very small. There are only chairs set up for twenty people. When Ethan gets there, I feel my brain melt, and when he sits next to me, I know that it's probably trickling out my ears.

"Are you nervous?" I ask.

He shrugs his shoulders. "A little."

"You'll do fine." I try not to sound so devoted. "I, on the other hand, will suck."

He laughs and shakes his head.

Was that funny? Oh damn, what's wrong with me?

"I've heard you play the piano," he says. "You're going to do really well."

"Am not! Look at my song!" I say, unfolding the four-page Mozart sonata.

His eyes widen. He's only been playing for a month or two. *Uh-oh, I didn't mean to intimidate him. Crap!*

But he smiles. "That's impressive," he says. Okay, my brains are officially a puddle on the floor. There's nothing left in my skull. Completely vacant. I feel the need to click my tongue like Natalia does in a room with high ceilings just to hear the sound bounce around the far-off edges. *Click, click. Click, click.*

Then the piano teacher is moving everyone, so the students sit in the order of the program. Ethan is moved to a chair a few yards away. He shrugs at me and talks to the gorgeous girl next to him. She bats her mascara-coated eyelashes at him and smiles with perfect white teeth.

Click, click. Click, click.

Sunday, December 25

It's four o'clock in the morning.

I wake up out of habit. Every Christmas Brodie runs screaming into my room right about now and tells me it's time to get up. I'd throw something at him. He'd leave, but not before my sleep was ruined. I guess he's finally grown out of it.

I'm almost disappointed.

It's times like these when family traditions mean the most to you.

. . . .

Three hours later Brodie and I jump on Mom and Dad's bed. "Wake up, it's Christmas!"

Dad grumbles something and rolls over. Brodie and I head downstairs.

The tree is lit, and even though the ornaments have been up for weeks, they seem especially gorgeous. Brodie and I go through our stockings (the only thing we can open until the whole family is present) and dump out our goodies.

Natalia comes down with Band-Aids all over her hands. Last night she somehow managed to break a framed picture of Jesus and was playing in the sharp fragments. There was blood all over. Fortunately after cleaning her off we could see that she only had cuts on her fingers, and they weren't too deep. It was not fun to clean up her room after the whole ordeal. Imagine Jesus looking out at you through splinters of wood, broken glass, and smears of your little sister's blood. Merry Freakin' Christmas.

Finally Mom and Dad come downstairs. We gather together, read Christmas stories, sing carols, and then start opening presents. We take turns, one by one, so that we can savor this once-a-year experience. I get a ton of books, classical music CDs, and some clothes. Mom also pays for all my make-up expenses as a gift. We eat a brunch of French Toast Casserole, omelets, and Mexican hot chocolate around eleven o'clock.

Brodie has been begging us for months to have a Family

Game Night, so as a Christmas gift to him, we all sit around the dining room table playing Clue. Brodie acts out his accusations using my game piece, Mrs. White (I always get stuck with the creepy maid).

"I believe it was Mrs. White with the wrench in the library," he says, trying to rip off Mrs. White's head with the miniature tool. He laughs hysterically.

We (minus Brodie) are all so bored that I pick up the little metal revolver and pantomime shooting myself in the head. For a murder mystery game, Clue is unnaturally dull. We finally guess and see who's closest. Brodie wins.

"Let's play Monopoly!" he shouts.

"NO!" We groan simultaneously. In comparison to Monopoly, Clue is Disneyland.

We end up playing Rummikub, which Dad wins. He does a victory dance which involves him pulling down the back of his pants to moon Mom. This would normally embarrass me, but Mom is sitting right in front of the open window, so that keeps everyone's spirits high.

> *Maya's Popularity Tip*
>
> Never invite friends over to Family Game
> Night, unless you have close contacts
> in the psychiatric profession.

All in all, it's been a wonderful Christmas.

. . . .

Monday, December 26

Ethan's parents invite us to their riverside cabin tonight for a barbecue and hot chocolate along with some other families. I'm so excited. And nervous.

I dress warmly and put on an extra layer of powder and lipstick to act as a shield against the cold. It's forty degrees tonight and I've realized that makeup serves as a great insulator. I'm really starting to like wearing it. It makes me feel different. Not necessarily more attractive, but more confident. Like I'm a secret agent. I enjoy putting it on.

As we drive I feel my heart race. I'm determined to talk to him.

When we pull into the driveway we greet everyone: a kiss on the cheek for the women, and a hug for the men. It's the way everyone says hello and good-bye down here. It makes you feel wonderfully close to perfect strangers.

I huddle in a chair and concentrate on staying warm. Dad sits next to me. All of a sudden, I feel a tap on my headband. I look up, ready to chastise Brodie for touching me, but instead *he* is there. Ethan.

Oh. My. Gosh.

I bite my lip and am pretty sure I get lipstick on my teeth.

"Hey there," he says, sitting on the opposite side of me.

"Hi," I say, trying to sound normal. I wipe my teeth with my sweater but the sleeve gets caught in my braces. I yank at it for a little while until the thread comes loose. I am so cool.

"Hi, Ethan," says Dad from his seat next to me. Ugh! I forgot he was there. I try to will him silently to leave, but as always, Dad doesn't (or won't) take the hint.

We talk a little about school, but all I can think about is the smug look on Dad's face. I glare at him. Oh, if looks could kill.

Finally, he gets up for an additional round of hugs and kisses as more friends arrive. Gratefully, his opportunity to ruin his daughter's life through embarrassment is gone. For now, at least.

I don't know if it's the cold or the fact that Dad's no longer watching me, but I suddenly find myself hardly able to control what I say. Tina Fey describes this phenomenon as "word vomit." So when Ethan mentions that the hot chocolate burned his tongue, I feel words come up my throat in uncontrolled heaves.

"When I was ten, my best friend made me hot chocolate, and she put it in the microwave for five minutes and of course I took a big gulp. I couldn't taste anything for a week. But she was nothing compared to the friend I had in fifth grade. She was the shyest girl in school. She had a wild home life. When I went over to her house, her uncle was slaughtering a porcupine on their front porch. There was so much blood and guts and it was disgusting—"

I clamp my hand over my mouth to prevent myself from continuing.

I swallow down the rest of the story (which goes something like this: When I got home that night I was really tired so I went straight to bed. Sometime after midnight my mom received a phone call from my friend's mother who told her I should check my crotch area for porcupine ticks.).

Ethan mumbles a "See ya," then gets up to go fishing. Feeling mortified by my oversharing, I watch him catch a shiny sheepshead. After he lets it go, it leaps into the air, and in the moonlight becomes the purest silver I've ever seen. With a swift kick of its tail, it falls into the black river where it disappears.

I get up to try and find some mint gum. I need something to get this acidic taste out of my mouth. Oh well. At least I didn't mention the crotch ticks.

~ Maya's Popularity Tip ~
If your mouth gets you in trouble,
flail your way into the nearest
body of water. I wish I had.

Wednesday, December 28

Brodie's convinced us to go to the beach even though it's too cold to swim. Instead of going out to South Padre Island, we make the longer drive along the Rio Grande down to Boca Chica Beach. The reason Brodie likes this beach so much is because, sooner or later, everything washes up here. We've found so many "interesting" things on past visits:

- A gunflint from the U.S.–Mexico War
- An orange oil rig helmet
- A dying pelican

- Lots and lots of shoes
- A fossilized horse tooth
- Several crusty bathing suits
- An inner tube filled with empty plastic milk
  jugs used by an undocumented immigrant to
  cross the river

AND...

- On one eventful day, a brick of marijuana
  wrapped in plastic

The beach extends all the way down to the mouth of the Rio Grande and you can wade across the shallow river over to Mexico. It is for this reason that we have to pass through a Border Patrol checkpoint. Our family's beach trips come complete with drug dogs and scary federal officers asking, "Mind if we check your vehicle, ma'am?" Usually though, all they want to know is your citizenship. Whenever we come here we play a very special game in the car. It's called, "What Not to Say When Asked 'Are you a U.S. citizen?'"

Here are our top five answers that would most likely get you taken away in handcuffs.

- Qué?
- I plead the Fifth.
- Is there a right answer?
- The question is, are you?

AND...

- I am, but I'm not sure about the two kids in the
  trunk.

Me, Natalia, and Brodie at Boca Chica Beach with half a boat we found

Thursday, December 29

I got burned at the beach yesterday. After a month of washing my face, not eating greasy foods, and closing my pores with ice cubes (freezing my face so badly my cheeks went numb)—none of which worked—it turns out the sun baked all the zits off my face. I now have perfect skin. Minus the flaking and redness of course.

I wonder if this is the "active outdoor life," that Betty was referring to. I have to admit, it's a little bit painful.

Saturday, December 31

It's the last day of the month, but more importantly, it's the last day of the year. We're all going over to the Montero's house.

Mr. Montero has made sushi, including vegetarian ones for me. I have on my powder, lipstick, and Vaseline. At the beginning of the month it felt like a mask. Now it just feels like me. It's become a part of my appearance. I don't jump back when I see my reflection.

The evening moves into nighttime at their house as I do homework on the couch. Mom has left early with Natalia who can't handle the noise of fireworks. As I'm finishing a holiday algebra work sheet, Ethan and his family come through the door.

He smiles at me, obviously forgetting (or choosing to ignore) the earlier porcupine story incident. I smile back, trying to seem composed and normal. We talk for a while and he teaches me and some of the other kids card games. He really is gorgeous.

Finally, it's time to go outside and light fireworks.

The sky is orange-gray with smoke. Dad stands next to me as someone begins a countdown.

"Ten!" *So makeup is over and I'm still not popular.*

"Nine!" *The paint on my face was hardly noticed (except by Kenzie).*

"Eight!" *But I think there's been a greater change.*

"Seven!" *It feels like I'm less afraid.*

"Six!" *I'm deciding now to be more confident.*

"Five!" *I'm going to be popular!*

"Four!" *And it's okay if I hit some stumbling blocks.*

"Three!" *Because I'll catch my balance and not give up.*

"Two!" *And whatever I'm doing will be fantastic!*

"ONE!"

All the couples at the party start kissing. Dad pulls me close into a big hug. I secretly watch Mr. and Mrs. Montero and I think that if I ever made out like they are, Dad would pop a blood vessel, and my lipstick would disappear before you could say, "Popularity, here I come!"

Fireworks blaze through the darkness, and gunshots echo through the night.

Happy New Year, Betty!

January

CLOTHES
& WHAT TO WEAR WHERE

I'm the type of person who runs away during uncomfortable scenes in books and movies. Not the racy or scary ones, but the situations that make your skin crawl with embarrassment. You know, when a character lies about being terminally ill to get out of jury duty, only to have it tailspin completely out of control as celebrities and international media get involved? I cover my eyes or flee from the room, thinking, "I'm so glad I'm not her right now."

But it's completely different now that my life has become that uncomfortable situation.

I can't leave.

Instead, I have to watch, however grotesque or painful it might be. I can't blame any director for his lack of judgment. There is only one person accountable for getting me into this mess.

Her name is Betty Cornell.

Well, okay, it's sort of my fault, too. I wanted to kick things up a notch for the new year.

But Betty's the one who has instructed me to wear a skirt and pearls to school tomorrow.

How did I let it get this far?

Monday, January 2

Brunettes . . . can play exotic in tangerine tones,
in reds, and in bright greens. They should be
careful of yellows that tend to give their skin a
sallow cast, but they can look to blues and beiges
with success.

Mom and I bought some clothes at the thrift store based on the wardrobe Betty outlines.

School:
  - *Several basic skirts in neutral shades*
  - *Long and short sleeved sweaters in classic colors*
  - *1 or 2 jumpers—a good dress-up-dress-down item*

I looked up the school dress code, and it allows khaki skirts with brown and yellow sweaters. It didn't say anything about jumpers. I'm not entirely sure what they are.

I still have to gather a few things.

Accessories:

- *2 or 3 pairs of nylon stockings*
- *2 pairs of white cotton gloves—for dress-up*
- *1 simple string of small pearls*

In the absence of jumpers, this morning (the first day back after Christmas break) this is what I wear: a knee-length khaki skirt, my yellow polo shirt (sorry Betty, but some dress code rules I can't change), and a brown, low-neck sweater. I stick my feet into the new (to me at least) black leather shoes. They have a square heel and a buckle on the top, like something a five-year-old would wear for a Thanksgiving pageant. I fasten Mom's pearls at the base of my neck and stare at my reflection.

It's literally painful. I look like someone out of an old movie, or a patient in a nursing home. Tears well up in my eyes, but I bite my lip. This is not the time for crying. This is the time to remember that I'm the protagonist in my own story, facing every challenge with grace and wit. I do one more makeup check, then walk slowly out the door. Mom wishes me luck, but I don't answer. Instead I listen to the *clop, clop* of my heels on the pavement. They are the drum-beats of my execution.

. . . .

The reaction isn't what I expected. I did get a few comments at lunch, but the whole experience feels somewhat anticlimactic. I wore a skirt for heaven's sake!

As flabbergasted as I am, I realize that Joshua, the eccentric kid in reading, came back from vacation with a beard. My strange new style simply can't compete with an overgrowth of middle school facial hair.

When I walk into science class, I do get some funny stares. One girl tells me I look fancy and my skirt is very . . . "Maya." I thank her.

> *Many people judge us by our dress. Clothes,*
> *being such obvious externals, are readily*
> *remarked* [on], *by anyone, and it is, indeed, often*
> *our tendency to think of our friends in relation*
> *to their dress. "That coat looks just like Mary" or*
> *"What a perfect skirt for Jane, just her type."*

My friend Dante stares at me and walks over. It's nice to see him again, considering the last time we interacted was when he wrote *Maya is flatulent. Ew!* on my notebook in permanent marker a couple of weeks ago.

"So," he says quietly, looking down at the pencil sharpener so that the teacher can't see him talking. "What's the big occasion?"

"Huh?" I say, like the straight-A student I am.

"Are you having pictures taken today?" he asks.

"Er, no. I'm just wearing the skirt . . . for fun!"

He laughs obnoxiously, and I'm reminded of how much he assumes the role of a big brother. The teacher looks up, pausing the lecture on physics that has meandered off to extreme cases of amusement park deaths. She raises her eyebrows.

"*You're a wild and crazy person*," he whispers to me sarcastically as he returns to his seat.

"I know," I say.

Meanwhile, Mr. Lawrence isn't back yet. I don't know what's going on, but I'm afraid to ask. What should I do?

Tuesday, January 3

Many kids at my school wear designer jeans and wouldn't be caught dead in Walmart-brand clothing. Even though we live in a poor community, they seems to find money to dress well. The required uniform still leaves room for self-expression and individuality, especially when the Volleyball Girl's polo shirts have giant designer names all over them. You can tell when someone spends money on their clothes.

> Being well dressed does not mean dressing expensively or lavishly. Many girls look well and fashionably dressed on very little money—they know how to pick and choose and they have sure sense of what's appropriate.

Thanks, Betty.

. . . .

Today I've decided to step it up a notch, try something a bit more challenging. As I get on the bus this second day of my clothing experiment, the lower half of my body shrouded in an ankle-length khaki circus tent, I'm surrounded by whispers and giggles. I miss Kenzie. If she wasn't lounging about in London, I know that she'd mock me too. But at least she wouldn't let anyone *else* mess with me.

By second period nobody looks me in the eyes. How can the length of your skirt affect your popularity so much? Be careful what you wish for: I wanted a bigger reaction and I got it. It's not a "Wow, she looks fantastic" reaction. It's a reaction that makes my face turn beet red and wish that I could crawl under a rock. I walk into choir and notice some boys in the class are watching me. Their eyes drift from my lopsided breasts to below my waist. They don't stop looking. I shift from one foot to the other, extremely uncomfortable. This has to count as some kind of sexual harassment. One of them mutters something I can't hear, and they all laugh.

"Come on you guys, that's just mean," says one girl.

I try to look dignified but I feel hopelessly lost. Finally my mind rests on an image of the women who fought our government for the right to vote. I did a report on the Suffrage Movement for History Day two years ago. They wore long skirts. They changed the world. I sit up a little straighter.

Even if I'm the only one in school covered by billowing material, I can manage.

The final bell rings and I make my way out the doors leading to the buses. I trudge through the muddy grass, lifting up my skirt. A teacher catches my eye. I smile but he frowns at me.

"Do you belong to . . . one of *those* churches?" he growls.

"N-n-no," I stutter.

"Oh good," he says, clearly relieved. "I just saw the long skirt and assumed."

Off he goes on his merry way, leaving me stunned. Betty Cornell was right. People do judge you on your clothes.

Maya's Popularity Tip

Don't question your wardrobe choices based on someone else's religious intolerance.

"Guess what, Maya," Mom says when I get home. "I went downtown today." Downtown Brownsville has Chinese import shops, bars, strip clubs, craft and clothing stores. We usually go there for the *ropa usadas* (used clothing stores) before Halloween. They sell clothes by the pound.

Mom pulls some items out of a plastic bag: panty hose, imitation pearl bracelets, and every size of plastic pearl earrings imaginable. She passes the bag to me, and I look inside.

I blink several times, blinded by sheer terror. This can't be happening.

I see a pair of cotton gloves . . . and a white faux-leather clutch purse.

This is going to have to be part of my Sunday outfit. Along with one other element:

Don't forget that there are occasions when you must wear a hat. Church is one place that you cannot go bareheaded.

I already know which hat I'll wear. It's a little straw boater with a white ribbon that ties in a bow at the back. It started life as part of my suffragette costume, but I figure that it works for this purpose as well.

I wonder what Ethan will think?

Wednesday, January 4

An eighth grader died today at another middle school in our town.

Some people say that he took his own life. But I wonder if he anticipated what would happen when he brandished the gun he'd brought to school and refused to put it down.

All the other kids on campus were put on lockdown. They heard the shots go off, three in all. Each one aimed at the boy. The students hid under their desks thinking they would die.

But no, only the fifteen-year-old eighth grader was killed.

I wonder what it felt like, to look down at the body of a child lying in the hallway of a school. And to realize that the thing clasped in his hand was nothing more than a pellet gun.

As I lay crying in my bed, I think about how little my fashion worries really matter.

Thursday, January 5

As I climb up the steps to the bus, I see two purple-and-black tennis shoes under the seat. I leap to hug my friend.

"Kenzie! You're back! Oh my gosh, how was it?!"

She flinches.

"Well, are you going to answer me?" I ask, plopping down on the seat next to her.

"Where are your *normal* shoes?" she asks in her dangerously low voice.

"In the locker . . . why?"

"You're wearing *pearls* . . . and a *sweater* . . . and a *skirt* . . . and *stockings*."

Actually they're panty hose, but I'm not about to tell her that. She's already twitching.

My full 1950s outfit

"Yep," I say.

"Why?" Her voice is almost a whine.

"For fun!" The response is almost second-nature now.

"What the hell, Maya? You've become a lady!"

"Not all 'ladies' dress in 1950s clothes," I say.

"Exactly! You've become an *old* lady! Old, old, old! You look like a teacher! You could be Ms. Thomson's twin! Her twin! Do you have any idea how dangerous this is?"

"Why? Is someone going to make fun of me or beat me up?" I tease.

"Both!" she snivels dramatically and shakes her head. "I- I don't even know who you are anymore!"

"Oh, Kenzie." I smile. "I've missed you, too."

Friday, January 6

"You'll never believe what I picked up at the Louvre!" Kenzie says, pulling out a big book from her backpack. "It's pictures of all the paintings they have there. See, look, there's *The Virgin of the Rocks*, by Leonardo da Vinci." She flips the page. "And oh, I remember this one!" she says. "But, I don't get why the artist thought that two naked women pinching each other's nipples was interesting."

"What?" Ms. Corbeil says as she walks out into the hall. She looks at me and stops dead in her tracks. It takes me a second to figure out why her mouth is agape. It's my outfit, not the painting. I sure outdid myself today. I've got panty hose, a mid-calf length khaki skirt, pearls, Pilgrim shoes, and, best of all, a pasty yellow cardigan sweater.

Kenzie jumps in because my tongue is tied and my face is red. "She looks like a substitute teacher, huh?"

"I know! She looks more professional than I do."

Oh, this is bad. I've actually taken a big step down my school's Popularity Scale. Substitutes are at the very bottom.

Sunday, January 8

I wake up early to get all my stuff together for church. Betty Cornell says that we should learn how to take care of our clothes, which is why I did my own laundry yesterday. Mom seems excited. The only problem is that I shrunk a truly awesome purple wool sweater down to Natalia's size. Live and learn, I guess.

For my church debut today, I decide on a navy blue dress, hat, gloves, pearls, and clutch purse.

City officials have been driven to despair by the sight of young ladies traipsing up and down their town in short shorts and bedraggled dungarees (I looked the word up. I think it means jeans, but I'm not sure). Whether you realize it or not, some so-called "informal" dress is enough to make adult blood pressure rise to the boiling point. For Heaven's sake, have a little pity on others and a lot of pride in yourself; put on a skirt when you're shopping.

"Let me guess. You're in a play or something," says Ethan's little brother when we get to church.

"Nope, just wearing this for fun." For fun. That response has become my explanation, my motto, my catch phrase. I'm beginning to adore these words.

"Oh," he says.

Ethan looks at me for a long moment, but not in the way that I would hope. I get a lot of that nowadays.

I ask him if he knows the time.

"I don't know . . . but I really like your hat." He smiles genuinely at me.

"Thank you," I say, blushing, not worrying about it showing through my powder.

Now I'm actually glad that I wore this straw contraption on my head.

My hat

. . . .

Tuesday, January 10

The bus was running very late, so when I get to school I have to go to the attendance office to clear my tardy. My algebra teacher comes in with a female PE coach. They're discussing something about tests, when all of a sudden Ms. Physical Education looks at me funny, like she's just watched one of those extremely depressing animal shelter commercials.

I try to grin, but she looks away. Strange.

When I try to leave the office, she blocks the door. She's about a foot taller than I am with red braided hair.

She whispers down to me, "I hope this question won't make you feel weird, but what size shoe do you wear?"

"I'm sorry?"

"I noticed that your shoes are too big. I have some extras the girls have left behind in the locker room."

I look down at my Pilgrim shoes. The buckle stares up at me. I don't understand what she means. "No, I'm fine, it's okay."

My Pilgrim shoes and panty hose

"Sweetie, it's all right. You can keep them. What size?"

Holy cow! She thinks I'm homeless!

I feel my face go hot, and my hands begin to sweat. I wipe them on my skirt.

She bites her lower lip. I'm too horrified to find any words.

Finally, she sighs and shakes her head. "I don't want you to feel bad about my asking, okay? Anything you need, dear."

Close your mouth, Maya, try not to look so shocked.

But as embarrassed as I am, I'm deeply touched by her compassion and generosity. If ever someone were to need a pair of shoes, I hope that they meet a person as kind as her.

But then I realize my algebra teacher and several others heard our conversation. So, I'm back to feeling mortified.

Wednesday, January 11

Kenzie and I aren't even quite sure if this insanity is real. How can it be?

We have just witnessed the depopularization of Nadia, a Volleyball Girl.

This much we can confirm (assuming Volleyball Girl gossip is a reliable source):

"Nadia was like, so like, being a bitch."

"So everyone else, was like, 'whatever,' and got all pissed and stuff."

"She stopped hanging out with us, and suddenly everything was different."

Kenzie and I have also pieced together the following time line:

It started with the angry, screaming music blasting on her iPod. Then she began hanging out with Josefina and Flor, the leaders of the Goth Art Chicks. Out went the sparkly headbands and in came dyed black hair. From there, she burned all bridges with the Volleyball Girls. It was official. She wasn't going back.

The strangest thing yet is the fact that Nadia is actually talking to me and Kenzie. She smiles at us. Ten days ago she didn't acknowledge our existence. Now she remembers our names.

So what is going on? Does being popular mean that you have to be a "bitch" to everyone except for your "friends?" In which case, do I really want to be like that? Maybe there is another definition of popularity. There has to be.

Thursday, January 12

I can't take it anymore. I have to know what's going on with Mr. Lawrence. Is he really sick? So I ask the one person I can trust to not "childproof" the answer for me. My librarian.

"Ms. Corbeil, do you know what's happened to Mr. Lawrence?"

She doesn't meet my eyes at first, but finally she speaks. "He's in the hospital again. Stage four cancer."

My heart stops and suddenly it's like the earth has lost all sound. My thoughts are painful and sharp like daggers. I've watched enough trashy doctor shows with Mom to know what happens during stage four of any cancer. I get on the computer and sure enough, my conclusions are confirmed.

Mr. Lawrence is dying.

The rest of my classes are a daze. I'm not quite sure how I make it through the day. Kenzie looks at me funny and asks what's wrong. I give her a quick explanation, and she apologizes sweetly and gives me my space.

When Mom picks me up and I tell her what's happened, I can't hold back the tears any longer.

"He's dying," I sob. "He's dying, and nobody told me."

She pats my back and lets me grieve.

"I'm so sorry, baby," she whispers, "So sorry." We're quiet for a while before she speaks again. "Honey, you should write him a letter. You need to make sure he knows what an impact he's had on your life."

When we get home I curl up at my desk and write for hours. It's more painful than anything else I've ever had to write. Two measly pages to sum up two years' worth of mentoring, teaching, and helping me discover my passion. Two pages to tell him how he helped me to discover myself.

Mom describes how I feel: "wrung out."

I curl up on the couch, not thinking.

Sometimes it hurts too bad to think.

Sunday, January 15

Today is Kenzie's fourteenth birthday party at the local bowling alley. I'm even wearing pants, just so I don't embarrass her. I got the invitation last Friday, but Natalia promptly ate it, so I'm not sure exactly where we're meeting inside. I open the front door and look for Kenzie. The music is deafening and it smells like fried food and shoe spray. I don't see her. My heart speeds up a little. Where is she? I pull out Mom's phone that she lent me before I left. I open it and see the date. My heart sinks.

"Kenzie's birthday party was yesterday," I groan out loud.

I sink against the dirty wall of the bowling alley. I feel so bad that I can hardly move. That is, until I notice the creepy guy with the Virgin Mary tattoo and sweaty wife-beater staring at me from over his plate of greasy nachos. I hide in the girl's bathroom and try to pull myself together.

You are the worst person in the world. You deserve to die a slow and painful death. In India, those who were sentenced to die would have an elephant step on their heads. You should move to India! How could you do this to your best friend?

When I finally get home I stare at the phone and try to find my courage. I dial Kenzie's number with shaking fingers.

"Hello," I hear Kenzie's voice on the other end of the line.

"Oh, I am so sorry! I went to your party, but a day late. I'm such a terrible friend!"

"Uh, who is this?"

"Oh right, it's Maya. I went to the bowling alley tonight, and the Virgin Mary and an elephant! I'm so stupid! I understand if you never want to speak to me again."

I finish my blabbering and hear suppressed emotion on the other end of the line. *Oh my gosh, she's crying. I'm never going to forgive myself. Really and truly.*

Then I realize what I'm really hearing. She's laughing at me. "I'm sorry," she says between gasps. "It's just too funny."

"What?"

"Just imagining you there with all those people, all loner and stuff. Oh, it's awesome!"

After I give her all the details of my terrible evening, we hang up. Not before she asks me if I saw the hot guy at the desk. Which I didn't.

Kenzie is a really fantastic friend.

Tuesday, January 17

"Welcome to your first day of health class," Ms. Welch says from her seat behind the desk. Ms. Welch is a tall, boisterous woman with long black hair.

Kenzie and I glance at each other. This is the moment we've been dreading since starting eighth grade. The last weeks of this semester will be entirely comprised of sex education.

We turn our textbooks to page four as instructed, and Ms. Welch begins discussing the many factors of health: physical, emotional, and social. "Another factor in your emotional health is how you deal with the many magical physical changes that you go through during your teenage years," Ms. Welch says.

A collective groan rises up. There's nothing worse in the world than an adult talking about "magical physical changes."

"I'm serious," Ms. Welch says, raising her eyebrows and

throwing her hands up in the air. "When you girls are on your periods, it really does affect your emotional health."

The guys snort. I feel my face go red. Ms. Welch barrels onward. "Oh come on, if you boys were feeling bipolar and had to change a bloody pad five times a day, I don't think that you'd make fun."

Their eyes go wide. I am so glad Carlos Sanchez isn't in this class.

"Anyway, it doesn't end there. Later in the year, we're going to watch a video on STDs, and we will actually observe different diseases on the penis and the vagina. I swear, boys, your penis can look like a piece of cauliflower."

By the end of class every girl has her legs crossed so tightly it would almost be funny if it weren't so disturbing.

Ms. Welch is the most effective teacher I've ever had.

I will *never* have sex. *Ever.*

Friday, January 20

Since I'm halfway through the school year, I will now take stock of how I am perceived:

TEACHERS: "Well behaved and dedicated."

GOTH ART CHICKS: "She's . . . weird."

FOOTBALL FACTION (mainly Carlos Sanchez): "Nerd."

LEON: "Beautiful."

LIBRARY NERDS: "She's nice, I guess."

CHOIR GEEKS: "Nerd."

BAND GEEKS: "Nerd."

KENZIE: "Epic Loser. Epically."

SUBSTITUTES: "I must find a coupon for where she shops. Where *did* she get that cardigan?"

Saturday, January 21

"You have to call Mr. Lawrence," Mom says, handing me the phone number. I sink into the kitchen chair. I hate making phone calls. It doesn't make things easier that now I have to call my favorite teacher in the world who is dying of cancer. Life isn't fair sometimes.

I exhale slowly. "Okay."

The phone rings five times and I prepare to leave a message. Then he answers. "Hello?"

"Hi, this is Maya," I try hard to sound cheerful.

"Oh hi, Maya." His voice is happy. "How are you doing?"

"Good, and you?"

"Not fantastic, but I'll be okay. As you probably heard, I've been recuperating from cancer."

"Yes, I've heard," I say, biting my lip. "Can I visit you? I'd like to show you some of my writing."

Mom smiles at me when I get off the phone.

"What's up?" she asks.

"I'm telling him about Betty Cornell. Tomorrow."

She shakes her head. "No, Maya, you can't. If word gets out that you're doing an experiment, everything you've done this year would be for nothing."

"This may be my only chance. He won't tell anyone."

She sighs and shakes her head. "It's *your* secret."

. . . .

Sunday, January 22

Mr. Lawrence lives in a beige house with a ceramic gnome on the front porch. "Ready?" Mom asks.

I nod, my fingers clasped tightly around the vase with the yellow rose and the envelope full of my recent short stories and poems. At the very back is the letter I wrote for him. Under that is hidden *Betty Cornell's Teen-Age Popularity Guide.*

I'm wearing a knee-length skirt with a blue blouse and my old lady shoes. No pearls or nylons. Or makeup. I want him to recognize me.

When I knock on the door, his wife answers. She brings us upstairs to Mr. Lawrence. He looks exhausted and has lost a lot of weight. He talks a little bit about his family and grandson, although he has trouble remembering what grade he's in. He tells me he misses teaching, except he can't recall who's covering his class now.

Finally he asks about writing. That's when I tell him about Dad finding Betty's book and about Mom's idea. I tell him about Kenzie and Carlos Sanchez. I tell him about my chapters.

I ask him to give me a quote about popularity so that I can use it in my book. He smiles and says he will.

When I leave, I say good-bye and promise to e-mail. I'm unsure if I will ever see him again.

The last words I hear him say are to his wife. His proudest voice echoes down the stairs and into my heart, "She's going to be a famous author someday."

. . . .

Monday, January 23

Today during choir, Nadia (Volleyball Girl turned Goth Art Chick) walks in with a new piercing at the top of her ear. She collects quite an audience of seventh graders as she shows it off. "When they pierced my ear my hearing changed," she says seriously. "Now I can talk to God . . . and Gandhi."

Her listeners nod gravely. It's no surprise that last year they were gullible sixth graders.

She walks up to me and stares at my outfit. I observe hers: black shoes, black earrings, black hair, black jeans, and a yellow polo.

"Wow," she says. "You look . . . pretty. Wait . . . No. Not pretty . . . Conservative. That's the word. You look *conservative.*"

I stare down at my outfit. Yellow old lady cardigan and Pilgrim shoes.

She's right.

"Does it make you smarter?" she asks.

I tell her I need to think about that. Later, even Carlos Sanchez compliments me.

"Hey, Maya. I am *enjoying* your sweater."

Ew. I have no idea what he means by that, but the way he says it makes me feel the need to scrub my brain out with bleach.

"I like your necklace," he continues.

I touch the strand of pearls at my collarbone. "Er, okay."

"It's kind of funny," he sneers. "My *grandma* has one just like it."

The class erupts into laughter.

. . . .

Friday, January 27

After finishing our Emotions collage Kenzie and I pass notes in health class discussing tuberculosis. Suddenly she drops her pen on the desk and smiles deviously. "I'm going to ask Ms. Welch about sexual things. Later loser." I watch as she casually strolls across the room to where the teacher is grading papers. She says something I can't hear and Ms. Welch's jaw drops. The woman mutters something unintelligible. Kenzie sits back down, content.

"You have no limits, Kenzie," I say. "There is never a dull moment with you."

"I know."

. . . .

Ms. Corbeil calls me over to her library desk, her cell phone in hand.

"Mr. Lawrence called and wanted me to ask you about a quote?" she says, confused.

I freeze.

"He couldn't remember which class you needed it for. What should I tell him?"

He's losing his memory. He's slipping away. My heart breaks. At the same time, I'm terrified. What if someone finds out about this project that I've been living for five months? It could all be over in an instant.

"It's okay, I can e-mail him," I say, pausing. "Um . . . It's for church, so there really isn't a time limit." My voice shakes, but I push through the lie.

Ms. Corbeil stares at me for a long moment before she turns her back. I can tell she's suspicious.

Tuesday, January 31

It's the last day of the month. I wear my long pioneer skirt that hits my ankles and my turtleneck sweater. Nobody whispers. Nobody looks at me funny.

"Do they like my outfits now?" I ask Kenzie as we leave health and walk through the schoolyard to get to our next class.

"No, you're still a loser," she states, pushing me in front of her to serve as an I-am-texting-and-don't-want-teachers-to-find-out barrier.

I sigh and realize she's right. I'm not popular. I am a loser. I make my way to choir and that's when I see it.

Across from me, standing there as cool as can be is a semi-popular Choir Geek. And on her neck is a strand of pearls.

A glimmer of hope in a dark and unpopular world.

At a choir concert wearing pearls

February

GOOD GROOMING
& AWAY FROM HOME

· ·

*In fairy tales, Prince Charming may have
discerned Cinderella's beauty under the soot
and ashes, but the chances are against a modern
young man poking through layers of dirt to find
his own true love.*

The first time I ever witnessed popularity was when I was
eight years old. There was a girl named Vanessa. She had to
have spent hours on her clean, organized appearance every
morning. And, of course, the guy I had a crush on at the time,
Jason, was in love with her.

I'd stand in front of the mirror and look at myself judgmen-
tally for hours trying to figure out the differences between her

and me. She was thin; I was chubby. She had smooth skin; I had a unibrow. She had new, pressed, clean clothes; I wore stretch pants and hand-me-downs. She had guys follow her home; I had the neighbor boy who would throw naked Barbies into our lilac bush. Vanessa was perfect. How could I measure up?

She was just so . . . put together.

This month I will strive to be more like Vanessa. I will iron my clothes. Bathe or shower daily. Keep my nails trimmed and my legs shaved. Take care of my unibrow. I will follow all of Betty's advice on how to be neat, tidy, and completely changed from my slobbish self. If the saying "The devil is in the details" holds true, then this is where the real transformation begins.

Thursday, February 2

Nobody wants to book a girl with dirty fingernails or a torn blouse. And certainly nobody wants to work with a model who stints on bathing and doesn't use a deodorant.

Kenzie and I stand outside waiting for school to start. My wardrobe has changed again for this month's theme. I've moved from rumpled skirts to ironed pants and spotless sweaters. My hair is slicked back in a neat ponytail. My Pilgrim shoes are shined.

All leather goods need to be polished—a little elbow grease and some wax will work wonders and make the leather last longer too.

When I point this fact out to Kenzie, she snorts. "What kind of a loser polishes her shoes?"

. . . .

I wear the same outfit to the church youth activity tonight. Liliana gives me a strange look but says nothing. I try to ease the mood with light conversation about the book I'm reading, which happens to be *The Hobbit*.

Ethan walks in and asks what we're talking about.

Uh-oh.... Here comes the verbal retching.

"Some girls at school and I do competitions on who can sound the nerdiest," I spew forth. "You see, one girl is a big follower of *Star Wars*, and another does *Star Trek* and now I'm reading *Lord of the Rings*." It's all true. Two Choir Geeks and I started the battle a couple days ago. There is no definite winner yet.

Then like a God-sent messenger, the rational voice comes back to my head.

SHUT UP, MAYA! SAVE YOUR DIGNITY BEFORE IT'S TOO LATE, YOU IDIOT!

"What do you mean 'sound nerdiest'?" he asks, his beautiful forehead wrinkling.

I heave again. "Well, we nerd-talk. You know, try to describe major plot points in the geekiest way possible."

"I still don't get it."

I try to swallow. I try to stop myself. But I've gone too far. "Let me demonstrate," I say with a stereotypical nerd voice. "There once was a Hobbit named Bilbo Baggins who lived in a Hobbit-hole in the magical land of Shire. He was very content smoking his long wooden pipe and eating several meals a day, but one day Gandalf, he's a wizard, came and invited Bilbo to join him on an adventure. Before he knew what was happening dwarves called Dwalin, and Balin, and Borin and Thorin (may his beard grow ever longer), and all these others took him on a big quest to go retrieve the stolen treasure from the dragon Smaug. On the way they stop at the house of Elrond and meet the Elvish folk . . ." I go on for about another Hobbit lifetime (well beyond a hundred years) until finally I'm left dry heaving and exhausted.

He walks away quickly.

I think I am going to die. Hobbits! I talked about HOBBITS!

Oh well. At least my shoes are polished.

Maya's Popularity Tip

Bite your tongue off before nerd-talking about *Lord of the Rings* to the boy you like. Unless he himself is from Middle Earth.

Friday, February 3

I can not overemphasize how necessary it is to be neat about what you wear.

I iron my capri pants, make sure my makeup is neat, and slick back my hair, long before the sun rises, leaving me plenty of time to ponder on my idiocy. Ethan will never like me. Maybe it's not so bad, dying alone. I could nerd-talk all I want and no one will hear me.

I pull on my pressed pants—or attempt to pull them on. I realize they are, in fact, my brother's trousers.

Obviously no amount of deodorant will ever mask the eternal stink coming from my clueless glands.

Sunday, February 5

"No. I will not be a part of this."

"Mom, tonight is our only chance."

"No, we are not buying you a girdle." She folds her arms and sits down on the couch. Her lips are pressed together in a tight line.

"Let her do it," Dad says. He seems to be making more of an effort to be patient with me these days. Yesterday I curled up next to him on the couch and we talked for an hour about school. He actually listened instead of lecturing.

"See, Dad supports me!" I argue.

"Your father's not himself. He's trying to *relate* to you." She glares.

"It's true. You might as well call me Michael," Dad murmurs from where he sits reading.

"Okay then. Michael supports me!"

We stare each other down until Natalia wanders in using her toy, Turtle, as a telephone for an imaginary conversation.

Finally, Mom gives in. We get into the car and rush to the mall in an attempt to reach it before closing time.

*I am firmly of the opinion that almost every teen
needs a girdle—not a whaleboned ironclad trap,
but some sort of lightweight affair to control the
curves. . . . Don't turn up your nose at the idea
of wearing these modern aids to figure beauty.
Today's girdle is a far cry from the cantankerous
corset Grandmother wore. Nowadays a girdle is
so light you scarcely know you have it on . . .*

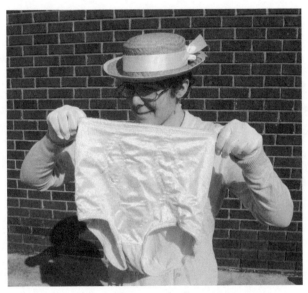

My panty girdle

. . . .

Ha! The girdle I'm trying on at the moment is so tight that it
makes my brain swell, not to mention my thighs. I try on four
or five before finding the least repulsive one: a beige panty
girdle with embroidered flowers. It's rather snug, but gives

me more of an hourglass shape than I ever thought possible. Hmmm.

After we leave the dressing room and it's clear I won't be talked out of my mission, Mom finally changes her attitude. We have fun and joke around as we smell the perfumes.

In addition to deodorants, you should get in the habit of using a light scent—any flower cologne will do, provided that it is fresh and fragrant.

With Mom's help, I pay for the girdle along with a bottle of Lilac Blossom Body Spray, the best "scent" I could find.

It's nice having Mom back and not the angry monster that momentarily possessed her. I'm guessing that her blood sugar was low. We probably should've bought some marked down doughnuts instead.

Tuesday, February 7

We've been working nonstop for the choir performance this week. We will be taking a bus almost three hundred miles north to San Antonio for a music convention.

Ms. Charles, the choir director, has been busy managing all the details.

"All right, girls," she says, taking out a clipboard, "who are you sharing a bed with at the hotel?"

Everybody giggles and starts making that very distinct

middle-school-girl sound—somewhere between a cheer and a shriek.

Ms. Charles goes down the list.

"Marina?" she asks.

"Victoria!" Marina squeals and the two start laughing.

"Nadia?"

"Selena."

I don't know what I will say. Beads of sweat start dripping down my face. It must be unusually hot in here.

> *If you perspire from nervousness, as many do,*
> *don't be alarmed, it is just a normal bodily*
> *reaction. . . . If you feel the necessity sew*
> *protective shields in your blouses and dresses. . . .*
> *An ounce of prevention is worth a pound of cure.*
> *A date once made uncomfortable or a friend*
> *offended by your carelessness will take a long*
> *time to forget.*

Thanks for the cleanliness insight, Betty, now get out of my head!

I bury my face in my pressed skirt. The names continue on and on until . . .

"Maya?"

"I-I-I don't really have anybody . . ."

"Well there are only four girls left. Leslie, who do you want to be with?"

Leslie glances at me. "Tina!"

Last person picked . . . last person picked. . . . That isn't popular. That's just sad.

I have to share a bed with someone I've never talked to before. I can't imagine how she feels about it.

Thursday, February 9

It is 5:00 in the morning and bitter cold as we wait outside in front of the school for the fancy transportation to arrive. Because our district doesn't have to pay for it, we get to stay in swanky hotels and ride buses that look more like airplanes. It's very, very cool.

Of course, first we have to line up all our bags end-to-end in the parking lot. I know that it's only procedure, but I can't help wondering if we're the only middle school that has to have our luggage sniffed by drug dogs before going on a field trip.

The police officers take the hyper beagle up and down the lines of backpacks and suitcases, while we're made to stand fifty feet away. I don't like drug dogs. Sadly, though, when you live in "Borderlandia," you get real familiar with seeing them.

Since no one signed up to be my "buddy" on the trip, I'm forced on Eva, a seventh grader, whose best friend got the stomach flu and couldn't come. We sit next to each other in silence at first, but we break the ice and talk for a while. I can still tell she's sad that her friend isn't there instead. At least I know I don't stink.

. . . .

Friday, February 10

The alarm on the side of the bed blares, and I smack the button. Slowly I creep into the bathroom and look at my reflection. Nope. No permanent-marker mustache. I smile. Maybe this trip won't be so bad after all.

I shower quickly and put on my girdle before anyone can see. I gargle with mouthwash as Betty requires, then rush to wake up the other girls.

When we're all dressed and ready, we get on the bus and drive to our concert. My heart beats loudly as we walk to the convention center. We do one final run-through and then are led silently to the risers at the front of a massive room filled with hundreds of people.

There is something really special about performing. From the moment Ms. Charles raises her hands, there is an anxious silence as the crowd waits. As we sing our first note, we notice the intake of breath in the audience. It's magic. I sing like I never have before. I'm so happy to be alive, to be here, in spite of all the awkwardness. I smile as Ms. Charles's hands dip and twirl. The music soars perfectly. I keep waiting for her to stop us because we forgot a staccato or to tell us that we're off pitch, but she leads us on. The bright lights keep us from seeing the audience so it feels as if they don't even exist. It's just the choir, the conductor, and the music.

All too quickly it's over.

The entire audience stands up. The applause is deafening.

. . . .

"All right, everyone who's skating, line up over there so that I can get you your passes," says Ms. Charles. Mom and I decided earlier that I was not going ice-skating with the other choir girls after the concert. I have incredibly bad knees, and that combined with my lack of coordination is a recipe for disaster. Mom even made me wrap my bad knee this entire trip just to be safe.

I sit down at a table outside the rink, parking myself near the window and pull out a book. After about twenty minutes, I look up and notice a growing cluster of concerned people. They peer down at the ice near where I am reading. I can see that it's Isabella, a seventh grader in our choir, sitting there.

I watch as the workers from the rink roll a wheelchair to her location. Isabella tries to stand but collapses. She fights back tears as they roll her into the room labeled MEDICAL AS-SISTANCE.

I try to read my book, but her pain is all I can think about. It's all-consuming and I watch the door until it opens. Isabella limps out holding an ice pack to her leg. She carefully seats herself a few tables over.

I'd never so much as said hello to Isabella. But, I just get up without even thinking about it and sit down next to her.

"Hey. Are you okay?" I ask gesturing at her knee.

"Yeah," she says, smiling halfheartedly. "I feel like such a loser. I was just starting to get good and then my knee went all crazy. It like popped out and then went back. It was really weird. Gosh, it hurts."

We talk for a little while about everything from injuries to musicals, to the fact that she wants to write novels. I give her my Ace bandage and show her how to wrap her knee.

After skating for another hour, our choir leaves to go back to the hotel. I help Isabella on the bus and off again. As we stand outside the door she says, "Thank you, Maya." Her eyes are full of tears. "Thank you for everything."

What is this newfound friendship? What does it mean for popularity? The crazy thing is, I never would have been confident enough to say hello before I began this experiment. Maybe real popularity comes from when you take time to listen to someone else. When you actually care about them.

Saturday, February 11

Isabella and I talk the entire bus ride home. We discuss clothing and style (apparently her favorite article of clothing is a skirt), food, and she even asks me for boy advice! Me, *Hobbit Girl*! Granted, most of what I say is "Wow," "Mmh," and "He doesn't deserve you if he acts like that."

The five-hour trip home is much nicer because the seventh graders now welcome me into their group. After they saw me being nice to Isabella, they started talking to me. All of them.

I hate to say it so soon, but maybe things can change. Maybe there's hope for me yet.

When Mom picks me up I tell her how it went. As supportive as she is, she didn't dare believe I could overcome the stigma of being last picked.

Neither did I.

. . . .

Tuesday, February 14

Today is Valentine's Day. I hand out chocolates and cards to all my teachers. It's amazing how many truly phenomenal educators grace this border town. I also pass out candy to my peers, including Leon, who thanks me genuinely. In my generous mood, I even give one to Carlos Sanchez.

"Gee thanks, Maya." He smirks, swiping another valentine off my desk and "accidentally" rips it apart. "I appreciate it."

I don't think I'll get anything in return, (the last two years I've only received three valentines) but maybe my luck is changing.

. . . .

SIX! SIX WHOLE VALENTINES! SIX!

It's all so wonderfully popular that I can hardly breathe. It started with the sixth grader who I'm nice to in the library. She gave me a package of M&M's. Cards from two choir girls whom I smile at. Candy and a drawing from the girl I sat next to in art class last year when no one else would. Then some chocolate from a seventh grader I hung out with on the trip.

And when I thought that things couldn't get any better, Isabella approaches me with a butterfly card and a stuffed dog. I've never gotten a plush valentine before.

I realize something as I thank all of these people for their gifts.

I have been kind to each of them in the past.

. . . .

Saturday, February 18

Girdles really suck, in spite of the fact that they give me a flatter stomach. If it's too low, it's a muffin-top extravaganza. If it's too high, you have a wedgie that has to be surgically removed.

I've also recognized another problem that proves Betty Cornell's girdle theory wrong. I have diagnosed myself with it:

QUADRUPLE CHEEK SYNDROME

CAUSE: Badly placed elastic

SYMPTOMS: Bulges of butt where the girdle
  cuts off the circulation, resulting in what
  appears to be multiple bums.

CURE: Take off the curve control!

My butt has giant purple stripes across it, but at least none of my four backsides jiggle.

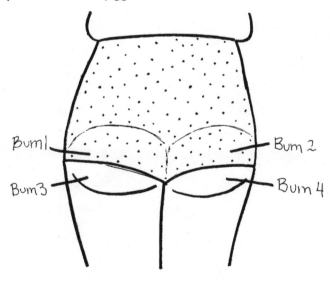

Sunday, February 19

I'm shaking as I walk into church today. I still haven't seen Ethan since the ghastly Hobbit Incident several weeks ago, so I'm terribly nervous.

I'm wearing clean clothes and my girdle, but I must admit that my confidence level is low. I checked my e-mail and found that my grandma had sent me a link about how to get rid of acne, so I spent thirty minutes washing my face. After that, I applied quite a bit of that body spray stuff. Maybe he'll notice.

. . . .

He didn't notice.

He did fall asleep during church, though, and when someone kicked him to sit up, he had a huge imprint of the seat in front of him on his forehead.

He's so dreamy.

I get up quickly to go to the bathroom as I feel the first heave of words trying to spew from my mouth.

It's a miracle that I get to safety before I can blurt out, "Your forehead looks just like my butt after I take off my girdle!"

Tuesday, February 21

All good grooming means attention to details. . . .
It means looking after yourself and your clothes.
It means hanging up your things when you take
them off—a skirt that has lain rumpled on the

*closet floor all night is not going to look like a
million dollars the next morning.*

I have completely reorganized my clothing and cleaned my
entire room. I've showered every day this month, endured
the girdle, worn perfume, learned how to apply lipstick better, made sure my hair didn't get frizzy and out of place, and
cleaned out my nails with an actual nail cleaner from a store.
My T-shirts are now arranged by color as well as by material.
Betty Cornell would be proud.

But today I feel like the only one who keeps up her good
grooming in this household.

Dad and Brodie walk downstairs shirtless. At least Brodie
is wearing pants.

Brodie drags Natalia into where Mom and I are making
dinner. Mom's not wearing a bra.

"Mom, Natalia smells. When's the last time you changed
her underwear," he asks.

"When's the last time you changed *your* underwear?" she
retorts.

He pauses and lets go of Nat's wrist. "Touché."

Wednesday, February 29

On the bus ride home from school, Kenzie sniffs my sweater,
which is clean and significantly coated in perfume. "You
smell . . . funny." I sigh. It's the last day of the month, and show-
ering daily and ironing my clothes hasn't catapulted me to the

top of my school's popularity scale. When I get home at the end of the day, I have a horrible red rash all around my waist from my girdle. Of course, Brodie mocks me for it and Natalia thinks it's funny to step on the red sores over and over again.

But this month hasn't been all bad. In fact, I have felt more popular than ever before. But it had more to do with kindness than keeping a wiggly backside in check. I find a box of fortune cookies hidden in back of the linen closet and crack one open.

GOOD LUCK WILL BE SHOWERED UPON YOU!

Gosh, I hope so.

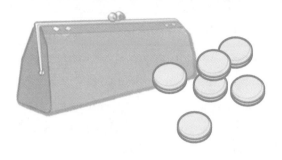

March

MONEY (HOW TO EARN EXTRA) & ON THE JOB

....

The plaintive lament about money or rather the lack of it cannot fairly be said to apply strictly to teen-agers. . . . However, teen-agers are in rather a special position in regard to money—they need more of it than children do and yet they are not free to earn it as an adult would.

Even though we are well-to-do compared to a lot of other people in Brownsville, I've never considered myself wealthy. I grew up listening to Mom and Dad's stories of sleeping on floors, pocketing food at film festivals, surviving off Ramen noodles, and saving up change to buy supplies for their next documentary. Although our lives have gotten a lot better since those days, my parents still worry about money. Mom bargain shops. Dad is always on the lookout for antiques to sell. He was a graduate student for years, believing that all that education would pay off financially once he got his Ph.D. I suppose he thought he would be making a lot more than he does now, which is less than my middle school teachers. I guess this is why we don't get an allowance.

> *Mothers and fathers do the best they can to provide for their offspring's needs, but when it comes to an extra formal or money for a froufrou blouse, things that aren't desperately needed but desperately desired, then the best answer is to try and earn your own.*

> *Baby-sitting can be a steady job or a hit-or-miss affair, depending on the way you want to go about it. If you want to work at it regularly there is nothing to prevent you from making up a list of clients and keeping in constant touch with them.*

. . . .

It shouldn't be too hard to get someone to trust awkward me with their children, right? I'll make flyers to broadcast my babysitting services, and while I wait for responses, I can do odd jobs around the house.

My moneymaking goal this month: fifty bucks. Maybe then I'll be able to pay for some top-of-the-line girdle ointment.

Thursday, March 1

Dad walks through the front door. The look on his face is half fear, half excitement. He sits down at the kitchen table.

"They offered me a job. A university in Georgia offered me a job."

Mom, Brodie, and I gape at him, too stunned to speak. Our family has moved twice in my memory, always following the jobs Dad gets, but past experience doesn't make it any easier to deal with this new bit of information.

"I'm not going to make the decision tonight," Dad answers. "There are too many factors. We don't even know if we can sell this house. But they'd pay me twenty-five percent more than I'm making now." He runs his fingers through his long hair, clearly flustered.

Without a word, I go to the linen closet and bring out the box of fortune cookies. "You need to ask the cookies, Dad. They know all." He laughs and picks one out. I sit down on his lap and watch as he opens the red-tinted cellophane.

"Okay, so this *dessert* will determine whether or not we move," he proclaims.

I put my hand on his wrist. "Trust the cookie." He cracks open the light brown shell and pulls out the scrap of paper. His eyes widen. I grab it from him and read:

YOU WILL TAKE A CHANCE AND BE GLAD YOU DID!

"I told you!" I gloat. I dance around the room, thrilled to have been right.

"It's not official!" Dad groans, exasperated.

We're moving! We're moving! Ha-ha!

All of a sudden, reality sets in, and it feels like my heart has been ripped out of my chest. I can't say good-bye to this place, to these people—Mr. Lawrence, Isabella, Dante, Leon, Ms. Corbeil and the Fishbowl. Even Carlos Sanchez's inane questions, his irritating laugh, and his gay pigeons. I'm going to miss him too.

And then it hits me . . .

Kenzie! Holy cow, how will I leave Kenzie?!

Sunday, March 4

At church today Liliana and I teach a lesson to the five-year-olds' class as part of a service project. If this were a wrestling match (which it kind of is), the headline would read: TEN DEMON CHILDREN VS. TWO UNPREPARED GIRLS.

If I'd seen the odds, I would've bet against me too.

Their ringleader, Sandy, never stops running around. While Liliana is trying to share a message about Jesus, I have Sandy on my lap, attempting to keep her from biting or screaming. She makes up a song about pooping. A regular Kenzie in training.

I made flyers to broadcast my babysitting service, but only

got to hand out three today. It's probably better that way. After today's experience, I will definitely be careful about where I advertise.

Monday, March 5

Dad obeys the fortune cookie and officially accepts the job today.

I go back and forth between wanting to vomit and wanting to soar up through the ceiling. Fear and excitement. Sorrow and curiosity.

During lunch, Kenzie and I talk. I try to avoid bringing up the subject of major life changes and instead ask her if she's excited for Spring Break. I haven't told her yet. Every time I try to, I end up at a loss for words. It's impossible.

"How could I be?" she groans. "My mom is sending me away to camp for the whole week," she mumbles.

"Well, camp can be fun, I guess," I'm trying to be positive. "What are you going to be doing?"

"I have to ride on a tour bus with a bunch of other Korean kids," Kenzie groans, laying her head down on the table. She whimpers, "Our moms organized the whole thing."

"Ouch. So, are you touring Texas?" I offer her half of my banana, which she accepts gratefully.

"Pennsylvania," she sobs through bites of fruit. From the way she says it, Pennsylvania might as well be synonymous with Purgatory.

"I am so sorry."

"And then we have to see the play *Jonah and the Whale*." Her voice cracks.

I bite my lip to keep from laughing. "That sounds awful!"

"Please tell my mom that. I even cried when she told me, but she had no mercy."

I feel so bad for Kenzie.

Still, it's very funny.

~~~ *Maya's Popularity Tip* ~~~

Laugh at your friends' painful situations
only after they give you permission to do so . . .
or when no one else is around.

Even though I laugh, deep down the secret eats me alive. We're moving. She's my best friend, and I don't even know how to tell her. I can't.

What if she cries? What if she doesn't? How can I handle it either way?

Tuesday, March 6

They appear today. The boxes. We're not moving until July, and they're already here, shoving their way into my life.

And yet, there's a sense of excitement in the air, a charged energy. It reminds me that there's a new adventure on the horizon.

Then again, the whole business kind of scares the girdle marks (yes, I still occasionally wear my girdle) off my four butts.

I'm so confused I seek out the wisdom of a fortune cookie.

YOU WILL BE SUCCESSFUL IN
YOUR FINANCIAL ENDEAVORS.

I'm beginning to think that these things are magical. I check my e-mail, but no one has contacted me about my babysitting services yet. Next Sunday I'm going to have to cast a wider net. Oh, boy.

> *There is yet another approach to the art of having enough money, and that is cutting down on expenses—or in the plain parlance of platitudes, "A penny saved is a penny earned." . . . ride a bike instead of the bus, write letters instead of making long distance telephone calls, and stay at home and play records instead of feeling obliged to see every movie that comes to town.*

Okay, Betty, I'll do my part to keep from spending my money on jukeboxes and pinball machines.

Wednesday, March 7

The hallways of our entire school are covered in lockers, but we aren't allowed to use them because of concerns over drugs and weapons. Instead, the art teachers display their students' projects all over them. As Kenzie and I walk slowly down the hall together we pass the dead pandas and vampire punk bands the Goth Art Chicks have drawn. I see Hello Kitty being swallowed up by a black hole, and I think I know how she feels. I can't hold back any longer.

"Kenzie, I have to tell you something. You're my best friend. You need to know first."

The smile disappears from her face. "What?"

"I'm not going to the same high school as you."

"What do you mean?" Her voice is soft and sad.

"Oh, Kenzie, we're moving this summer. My dad got an amazing job in Georgia. It's a nice place and all, but I'm going to miss you so much."

She looks away. I stare at the rows of empty lockers.

Finally, Kenzie looks up. "You'd better Facebook me."

"All the time," I reply.

We sigh and stand there for a while. The bell for first period rings, and we give each other a sad smile. I walk quickly to algebra, filled with pain and relief.

The principal's voice bursts out over the intercom. "Students, I must inform you of a sad event. Mr. Lawrence, one of our seventh-grade English teachers, passed away this morning."

I look up. *No. NO!*

"Funeral information will be given at a later date. We will now have a moment of silence to honor the life of such an amazing teacher. . . ."

All first period, I'm in a daze. *It's not real. Not real. He can't be dead. He's my mentor, my friend. NO!*

After class Kenzie grabs my arm in the hallway. Our eyes meet and I see compassion like I've never witnessed before.

"Maya, I'm so sorry," she says, pulling me into a hug.

"He's dead," I sob into her arms, leaving wet spots on her jacket. "He's dead."

"I know," she says.

We stand like that for a long time, and in that moment, I know that Kenzie will never abandon me. We're two outsiders who don't quite fit in anywhere, but together find a place to belong. No matter where we are or what happens, she'll always be my friend.

We pull away, and I see the tears in her eyes too. Silently we leave for our classes: me to choir, her to band.

By this time the emotions are flowing freely down my cheeks, and I can't stop them.

Dead. There it is again, that strange, impossible word. I can't wrap my mind around it. I hug my arms around my shoulders and cry silently into my knees. I'm not the only one. Several other girls are sobbing into their boyfriends' arms. How dare they cry! So many of them gave Mr. Lawrence a hard time when he was alive.

My feelings change though, as unfamiliar hands reach out and pat my back. The seventh graders all gather around and hug me, telling me how sad they are. People hand me tissues and run loving fingers through my hair.

I wonder if I should feel popular, but all I feel in numb. No popularity exists when tragedy strikes. All that's left are human hearts and love and ache. We all love each other, deep down, and when we see another soul in pain we can't help but hurt too.

I find my peace in the arms of total strangers who have never spoken to me before. In third period, I see Carlos Sanchez, red-faced, hiding his tears as he defensively states that girls crying makes him "feel weird."

This is universal love, found in the most unlikely place.

This love is what keeps me going through the day, until I collapse into my mother's and father's arms and sob.

Thursday, March 8

At school today I feel as if everybody else has moved on. There are no more girls crying, so I save my sadness for when no one is around.

I go home and listen to the first CD I find in my closet, which happens to be ABBA. I lay down on my bed and cry. I don't want anyone to see. This isn't the dramatic sadness that I'm so used to. It's too hard to admit that deep down I am broken, caught in a continual ache that doesn't go away. I sob into a pillow, nodding my head along to "Money, Money, Money." (Doesn't that theme just keep recurring?)

I have to grieve on my own. Work through it in my own time.

Nobody has contacted me about babysitting. I guess that I'm not going to make any money this month.

My family has been going through boxes of papers and folders. Brodie finds twenty bucks left in his old birthday cards.

I look through tons of stuff and retrieve nothing.

. . . .

Saturday, March 10

A fitted white blouse.

A black skirt.

A pair of black flats.

A big black coat that belongs to Mom.

The funeral home isn't far away. Mom parks the car and we walk through the rain and into a little chapel full of hushed talk. On a large screen over a closed casket covered with an American flag, they play a slide show of pictures from Mr. Lawrence's life: him with his grandchildren, his wife, his students.

I sit and listen as Mr. Lawrence's sons tell stories about him and remind us of the things that he stood for. He always saw the best in people. He had so much courage. He was kind and loved his students so very much.

Tears stream down my face as we sing "Amazing Grace" and everyone gets up to pay their respects to the family. When I approach and tell them my name, they all smile. His wife hugs me, and all his sons shake my hand.

"I want to thank you for writing that letter," the eldest says. "It meant the world to him."

"He was always so proud of you. So proud."

"So, you're Maya. He adored you. I have a framed copy of the poem you wrote for him on my wall."

"Thank you *so* much. You made such a difference for him."

I'm so overcome I can hardly speak.

Mom and I walk to the graveside where veterans perform a military salute. In the silence that follows the firing of guns, the funeral director thanks us for coming.

Before Mom and I leave, I make my way to his casket. I almost can't help but laugh at how small it is. How do you fit so much life into a seven-foot-long wooden box?

I rest my hand on the polished surface.

"How do I say good-bye to you?" I whisper, leaning in close. "You always told me I had a gift for words, and now here I am, unable to find any phrase that can tell you how much you mean to me. What made you believe in me?"

Tears stream down my cheeks as I remember the last words I heard him say: "She's going to be a famous author someday."

"Good-bye, Mr. Lawrence. Good-bye."

Mr. Lawrence, this book is for you. This book that you will never read.

I promise, I won't ever forget.

Sunday, March 11

During church, Natalia lines up all her Beanie Babies on the pew in front of us. One falls back, leaving a gap like a missing tooth. The man in the bench in front of us leans over to retrieve it. Nat rips the toy out of his hands.

"Say thank you," encourages Brodie.

Natalia looks the man straight in the eyes and does as she's told. Except, Natalia can't pronounce her *n*s, and the *Th* sound comes out like an *f.*

Betty Cornell doesn't give much advice about how to smooth over the situations created by an autistic little sister.

> ## ~ Maya's Popularity Tip ~
> When you have eccentric younger siblings,
> it is extremely important to learn the art
> of apology at an early age. You will need it.

I hand out some more babysitting flyers. Maybe something will come of it.

Tuesday, March 13

Mom and Dad go to a friend's house tonight and leave me to babysit for a couple hours. They even pay me ten bucks, getting me closer to my fifty-dollar goal. As a paid professional, I decide to spend some one-on-one time with Natalia instead of letting her watch *Wonder Pets* for far too long.

> *In order to amuse the children during the time that you are responsible for them, you could take them to the park, to the playground, or to the beach . . . On rainy days you could use your own home . . . and read them books and supply them with crayons and paints.*

Due to my lack of transportation options, I opt for the reading and art supplies. I watch as Natalia points to and identifies the illustrations in a book.

"Cat. *Meow!* Sheep. *Baa!* Cow (it's actually a horse). *Moooooo!*"

She gets almost all of them except for ladybug, but really, what kind of madman puts an insect in a book about farm animals anyway?

After that, I tell her it's time for bed. I try to tuck her under her blankets, but she refuses to go to sleep. "NO!" she screams until I'm forced to tickle her. She laughs and wants to return the favor. Natalia's tickles involve a lot of painful jabbing in the breast area so I'm not overjoyed to endure it, but she just giggles and keeps going. "Tickow?" she begs over and over. She really is adorable. But next time I'll wear one of those atrocious cone bras from the 1950s. Then she won't poke my boobs, for fear of being impaled.

Sunday, March 18

Two moms approach me during church and say they want to have me babysit soon. One actually gave me a DATE! I will watch two of her three kids on the thirtieth of this month. A little late, Betty, I know, but still better than nothing. I figure if I make a good amount I can reach my goal.

Wednesday, March 21

Some of the noteworthy things that happened today:

1st Period

"What's Caucasian?" one Basketball Girl asks. (Basketball Girls are about an 8 ¾ on My School's Popularity Scale, just below the Football Faction.)

"Oh, that's easy," answers a Volleyball Girl, "it means white and American. You know, a hillbilly."

3rd Period

Carlos Sanchez scrapes his desk on the floor, making farting noises.

4th Period

HEALTH EXAM! Ms. Welch, who's been talking loudly to a Volleyball Girl about boyfriend problems, suddenly tells us to clear our desks. "It's time for our testicle. Ooh, I mean test."

7th Period Lunch

Kenzie pulls out a fifty-dollar bill (one of three, she tells me) from her wallet, and goes to buy some "real food" at the snack bar. She gets a generous allowance. Kenzie buys two chocolate chip cookies and a bag of ranch-flavored Doritos. I have been careful not to spend my money on such frivolous things.

A way of saving that will repay you in other ways than cash in the bank is the curtailment of eating snacks between meals. With this method, five cents saved on a candy bar will also be 100 calories saved from settling on your hipline.

. . . .

Thursday, March 22

Francisco gets made fun of during lunch today. It's been happening more and more often since he came out last summer. I had no idea until Kenzie told me about it when we came back to school in September. I think it was so brave of him. Two Football Faction members sit on either side of his hunched shoulders. He's trying to make himself as small a target as possible.

"Hey, girlfriend! You have on some nice makeup today. It makes your eyes just sparkle," one says bumping into Francisco's shoulder.

"Yeah, where's your *boyfriend*? I'm sure he thinks so too," the other replies, laughing.

Francisco looks down. I want to yell at them, tell them to go away. They have no idea what they're saying. Still, I bite my tongue. Speaking will only make Francisco's position worse. Defended by a GIRL is the ultimate of lows. Boys have gotten beat up for that. So I stay quiet, trying to send him support through my facial expressions, but he doesn't look up. He just sits, staring at his hands while they torment him. They eventually run off, but it's so not right.

I hate the Football Faction.

Friday, March 23

Mom pays me five bucks to write a short poem to put in the party favors for a baby shower she's hosting tonight. It's not very good, but I get fifty cents a line. Not too bad. Adding the payment I got for doing odd jobs around the house, this brings my grand total this month to thirty dollars.

All I need is twenty more!

Friday, March 30

I fidget with the sleeve of my nice, clean sweater as Mrs. Blanco pulls up her fancy car to our house around six o'clock to pick me up.

"Be neatly and conservatively dressed for business," Betty advises. *"Good manners are one of the things employers notice right from the very start."*

I do my best to make polite conversation; after all, I want her to trust me.

I'm going to be babysitting her two children until nine thirty. Her daughter, Mary, is in first grade and her son, John, is in preschool. Because of the rate I included on my flyer, I already know that I'm going to make eighteen dollars tonight, almost enough to bring me to my goal.

When I get there, the kids rush toward me.

"Can we play board games? Chutes and Ladders? PLEASE?!" Mary hasn't even learned my name yet and she's already pulling me by the sleeve. In my (limited) previous babysitting experiences, you couldn't *pay* the kids to play a board game. This is too good to be true.

Mrs. Blanco laughs. "Okay, so they haven't had dinner, but just feed them whatever. Cereal is great. Oh, and they can watch TV, or do what they want. Bedtime is around nine-ish.

Whenever works. They're already in their pajamas."

Does she realize how easy she's made my job? Mr. and Mrs. Blanco leave. The kids decide they want to do a dance competition for me, but I have to scoop them off the kitchen counters so they don't hurt themselves while they groove. Mary finds a bottle of lotion, and she empties it into her hands. After I take that, she locates a can of Febreze and impersonates a fountain. I deal with the mess and make them ham sandwiches ("without the crust!") and some Goldfish crackers.

Then they ask me to read them a book.

"Why don't we make up our own?" I say. "I know a fun game that we can play. We each tell part of a story, and the other person finishes it. It's cool."

"What's that on your teeth?" John asks, pointing to my braces.

Mary rolls her eyes and says, "She ate too much junk food. Right?"

"Um, well actually, never mind. Anyway, let me just start a story."

So this is the yarn we spin.

MAYA: Once upon a time there was a little boy
and a little girl (I look meaningfully at
them and they giggle) and they went on a
picnic in the park. ("We've never been on
a picnic," Mary says.) *Shh*, listen . . . And
then it began to rain and rain and rain.

They hopped on a little boat and sailed
down the river. Okay, Mary, your turn. . . .

MARY: Well, they floated to their house, but a
robber was there. And he pulled out his
machine gun and shot and shot at them.
They ran inside and hid in a closet, but
he was still after them. He shot holes in
the front door, so they put all the heavy
furniture behind the door. Then he blew
it all up, so they swam away. John . . .

JOHN: So they swam and swam until they died.
The End.

I let them watch *Dora*. Good ole fashioned mind-numbing
TV ought to keep them from thinking about all that darkness
and death. Nine o'clock approaches, and I read them some stories, not even considering having them make one up again. I
take Mary into her room, tuck her in, and tell her it's time to
go to sleep.

"I can't."

"Why not?"

"I'm scared," she mumbles, her voice reaching three octaves
higher than its usual state.

"Of what?" I ask.

"I'm scared of Scooby-Doo. I saw a mummy, and he came
to life and chased after them."

"Oh." I nod. "But it was just a guy in a mask, right? It's never a real monster. Mummies don't come back to life."

"Okay . . ." she consents, laying her head down on the pillow. She sits straight back up. "What about zombies?"

"Zombies aren't real, either. Dead people don't wake up."

"Jesus did."

Good grief.

"That was different . . ." I begin, but then pause. I have to plan my next words carefully so she doesn't have nightmares about Zombie Jesus. "Um, he was . . . nice?"

"I'm still scared." She grabs my hand and gives me big, brown, puppy-dog eyes.

I tell her a happy story about rainbows and stuffed animals and she finally nods off.

Finally they're both in their own rooms, and I pull out a book. Seconds later the door opens and Mr. and Mrs. Blanco step inside.

"Wow! They're in bed? That's amazing!" Mrs. Blanco smiles at me, while I'm silently praying that those kids will go on pretending to be asleep. "So how much do I owe you?"

"Eighteen dollars," I say.

"Oh, well, let me just give you twenty!" Mrs. Blanco says.

That two-dollar tip pulled me up to my goal! Fifty dollars—I did it! I am self-reliant! I can do anything!

When I get home at nine thirty I skip around the house.

Sincerity, genuine interest in people, a natural
ease in conversation, honesty, all do much

to make a young person a truly delightful
individual—on and off the job.

With Betty's help, I've been transforming. Maybe I'm not that far off from being *"a truly delightful individual."* With a jingle in my pockets and a smile on my face, I stride confidently into my next chapter.

April

POPULAR ATTITUDE:
LOOK PRETTY—BE PRETTY
ARE YOU SHY?
& PERSONALITY

*If you want to be a human being, and a popular
human being, then you have to stop being an
oyster and come out of your shell.*

I know I say this every month, but I really don't think I can do
this. All the girdles and skirts are child's play in comparison
to this month's goal: tearing out my antisocial tendencies by
their roots.

When I was four years old, my grandma took me to a park
near her house. Now, my dear grandmother is a social butterfly. She makes best friends with the person in front of her in
the grocery store line, or with customer service representatives
in India. So she couldn't figure out why her granddaughter
had such a hard time meeting new people.

"Maya, go play with those kids over there. They look nice."

"No," I'd protest.

"Well, why not?"

"Because, I don't *like* the other children."

That statement has shaped my entire life.

Now Brodie, on the other hand, is his grandmother's grandson. He has tons of friends. How does he do it? Is it the hazel eyes that match his sandy blond hair? The dimples? Betty Cornell says not.

> Being pretty and attractive does help you to
> be popular, but being pretty and attractive
> does not and never can guarantee that you
> will be popular. There is another factor, a
> very important factor, and that is personality.
> Personality is that indescribable something that
> sets you off as a person. It is hard to explain but
> easy to recognize.

So how do you get that indescribable something? Betty has three chapters about it that I'm going to be following this month. They deal with manners, shyness, and personality.

> You see, good looks are not enough. In order to be
> a success in the world, you have to be pretty as
> well as look pretty. How do you get to be pretty?
> By having a pleasant personality. Sounds simple,
> but it isn't. For a pleasant personality means that

you must be affable, considerate, generous, open
hearted and polite, adjectives that add up to
good manners.

That's a lot to accomplish. And there's more.

The most basic of all the basic fundamentals
is getting along with people. You can't have fun
all by yourself. You need to share the pleasure in
order to really savor the sensation. That means
having friends.

Okay. I'll try. But there is only one place to meet people. Only one place you can watch the popularity scale in all of its horrific glory. And it's the most unforgiving, foul smelling, heart-wrenching place on campus.

The cafeteria.

Now I will have to leave the security of my little clan of Social Outcasts and venture out on my own. I have to go out and meet *new* people.

I'm going to do this by sitting with other groups at different tables every day. I'll start with people I know, move on to strangers, then finally face . . . the *Popular* crowd.

I think the most important thing about getting
over shyness is to do it by degrees. Start small
and work up.

All right, Betty.
Here goes everything.

Monday, April 2

I say "hi" to three people on the bus this morning, but they either ignore me or can't hear over the sound of their headphones. It's impossible to compete with Angry Birds.

I'm wearing regular clothes today. It seems more appropriate for the battle ahead.

> *By the way you look, talk and think you are*
> *identified as a modern American teen-ager . . .*
> *Just think how many changes have taken place*
> *in America since 1900 and how many will take*
> *place before 2000. . . . The trick is knowing how*
> *to adapt to changes and still maintain your*
> *own standards and your own individuality.*

I'm still putting on my pearls and makeup each morning, but I'm wearing pants again. Adaptation is good. Survival of the fittest, right?

I meet two seventh graders in the library before school. Morgan and Noah are nice, and I wave to them in the hall on my way to lunch. I guess that's part of it. To be popular I have to make an effort to maintain a friendship with the people I meet.

For this first day, I sit with my own regular, Social Outcast group during lunch. I listen politely to yet another story about how Kenzie's mother is stressing her out.

"Look, Kenzie, you know how I'm moving next year?" I say, when she pauses for breath.

"Mhm."

"Well, I want to meet lots of new people before I go. I'm going to sit at different tables, and say 'hi' to everyone. You know, make friends."

She chokes on her cookie.

"What the hell? You're going to break the status quo! Ruin the social ladder! Destroy all the things that hold this world together!"

"And?" I protest, pretending to be more confident than I really am.

"*And*, it's impossible! . . . Stop it! . . . Shut up!" She turns away from me.

"Kenzie, what have I got to lose?"

She pauses and looks right at me. "Damn girl! You've got *guts*!"

I nod and laugh to myself. "And I want you to come with me."

"*HELL* NO!"

I sigh. The hero must face the dragon on her own.

Tuesday, April 3

Today I decide to join another Social Outcast table close to ours. I wipe my sweaty palms on my pants. I can feel my heartbeat in my neck, and I gulp. This is it. Everything I've been working for this year. I can do this. I put my backpack down next to a group of people I sort of know. Adam, Emma, and her boyfriend, Bernardo, tell me they don't mind me being there, even though they seem a little confused as to why I left my table.

Kenzie informed my own little group of Social Outcasts about my plan to meet new people, and they were about as encouraging as she was.

"What the hell, Maya? Get your sorry ass back here!"

"Maya, don't do it! You're not strong enough! Come home!"

"Who the hell are you and what the hell did you do with the real Maya?"

"Please, you're not well! Come back!"

"Are you insane?!"

It's good to know that I have such a strong support system.

It turns out that Bernardo knew my name from when we were in the same sixth-grade English class. I have to admit, I didn't know his. Why didn't I ever take the time to learn Bernardo's name?

Wednesday, April 4

After a very convincing pep talk in the mirror, I sit with the Spanish Club at lunch (somewhere between a four and a five on the Popularity Scale). I know one person in the group, and we talk for a while.

Surprisingly, I find out that the other girls know my name, too. We chat for a long time about Georgia and new movies. Soon the language switches to Spanish, so I just smile and nod.

Maya's Popularity Tip

When there is a language barrier keeping you from communicating with people, make it seem like you know what's going on. You can also pretend to be greatly absorbed in what you're eating. Looking busy solves a lot of problems.

Thursday, April 5

During science I find myself daydreaming. Today, I sat with the eighth-grade Choir Geeks during lunch. I had a great time talking about the San Antonio trip. I'd always thought they were mean and judgmental, but I guess I was the one judging before I really got to know them. I liked hanging out with them, and I think they liked me too. I even gave one of them my e-mail address. Maybe I won't be the last one picked anymore.

Saturday, April 7

I sit down and finally take the time to sort through my very neglected e-mail account. I see that the choir girl who I sat with has sent me a goofy message. Hurray! Popularity in the making!

Then, buried at the bottom of the list under Facebook up-
dates and advertisements, I see an unopened e-mail. I click on it.

> Dear Maya,
>
> Outstanding work! I feel very positive
> about your stories and poetry. It's obvious
> that you really put your heart into them, and
> that is what really matters.
>
> Call me any time and we will talk about
> your quote, and don't forget, today is going
> to be a wonderful day!
>
> Very Sincerely,
> Mr. Lawrence

I stare at the screen for a long time before looking at the
date. January 30.

I print the e-mail, and curl up with the paper and cry.

Sunday, April 8

It's Easter morning, and there's a basket of goodies in my room
when I wake up. Even though I know a fluffy, white rabbit
didn't deliver it, chocolate is magical nonetheless.

We have church at nine o'clock, so we all scramble about and
get ready. I wear a new floral-print, thrift store dress, my straw

boater hat with the white bow around it, my gloves, white clutch purse, and pearls. Betty Cornell would definitely approve.

During Sunday School I sit next to a boy I've never talked to before. He's always been very quiet, but I know his name is Hector.

In the spirit of this month, I decide to break the ice. "So, Hector," I say, "you don't talk much."

"Not to you," he mumbles, shrinking away.

"Are you scared of me?" I look up at him, pretending to feel confident. Mom told me that's what you have to do—behave as if you're self-assured, beautiful, capable, and those feelings just might follow. I also read an article in *Oprah* magazine about how sitting like a confident person can actually make you feel stronger.

This whole "fake-it-till-you-make-it" mindset is nice and all, but it sure is hard. Especially when you're the only one willing to make conversation.

"You're scared of me, aren't you?" I say, inching my chair closer to him.

"Yeah."

"I don't see why," I say, pretending to be an actress, playing a part in a movie. I smile at the idea of my costume: braces, glasses, pearls, gloves, hat. I have to be the least menacing person on the planet.

"If you got to know me, I'm sure you wouldn't be so scared. Let's start with school. My favorite subject is English, what's yours?"

"History."

"That's cool. Do you have a good teacher?"

"Yeah."

I'm sweating like crazy, but I keep my face animated. "Sometimes you get history teachers that make you read out of the textbook all day. But that's not too bad. Once, I had an English teacher who didn't know who Tolkien was."

"Oh, yeah? My English teacher doesn't know who Edgar Allan Poe is."

"No way."

"It's true!" He starts to laugh, and suddenly, I'm not so anxious. We talk for a little longer, and then he leaves. I think I can count him as a new friend I met this month.

I've talked to lots of people, and I find out that most are actually shyer than I am. Some of them hardly speak back to me. I'd always thought I was alone in my suffering, but tons of other people are shy too.

> *Shyness is an experience that most of us have had at one time or another. Some of us get over it quickly, like the measles, but others find that it drags on and on like a bad cold.*

. . . .

It's only after I get home that I realize that Ethan wasn't at church today. It used to be that every time that he was there, I could acutely feel his presence every moment. Now, I'm so busy pretending to be confident that I don't have time to be distracted by him.

I guess he's different than he was.

Or maybe I'm the one who's changed.

I stare at the two girls who I've carefully observed and decided will be a safe bet for my next lunch adventure.

"Hey, can I sit with you guys today?"

"Um, I guess."

I plop my backpack down on the bench and pull out my paper bag lunch.

"I'm Maya, by the way. What are your names?"

"I'm Dulce," says the brunette. She's about the same height as a sixth grader and smiles continually. "And she," she points to her slender companion, "is Eleanor."

"Well it's nice to meet you. Tell me about yourselves."

They look at each other and start to giggle. I'm still awfully nervous, even though I've been doing this for nine days already. Dulce is sweet and laughs a lot, but Eleanor is guarded and leaves for the band room at the first opportunity she gets.

I realize then that Dulce gets left alone during lunch every day.

Kenzie comes to the table and asks me if I want to go to the library with her.

"Um, well," I look at Dulce, sitting alone. "I think I'm going to stick around here for a while longer."

Kenzie is flabbergasted. She knocks on my forehead. "Hello, there. Do you happen to know where my friend Maya went?"

"Oh stop it." I grin, waving her hand away. "You can join us if you'd like to."

She slowly narrows her eyes and sinks down on the seat.

"You are . . . insane."

Kenzie ends up staying, and we all talk for the entire lunch period.

I walk Dulce to her class and she smiles at me.

Is it working? Am I actually making friends?

Wednesday, April 11

Yesterday I went to the cafeteria early and sat at an empty table. Even though it's usually crowded, no one sat down next to me. After a little while two Choir Geeks came over.

"Look, Maya, do you want to come sit at our table? It's kind of crowded but we don't want you to sit alone."

I was touched by their kind gesture. And, having pre-decided to accept any invitations to other tables, I went willingly. But as nice as it was, I knew everyone there and didn't get to meet anyone new.

That's why today I sit with my own Social Outcast family. I really don't want them to think I'm avoiding them. Anyway, Kenzie is at a band competition so she can't give me lip about chickening out on my new endeavor and "crawling back to them."

. . . .

That evening I arrive a little late for a youth activity at church. When I walk in, I see that there's someone I don't recognize. She looks sad and out of place, and I feel awful for her. Without hesitation, I walk right up and sit down next to her. I laugh and talk, getting her to come out of her shell. I know how it feels to be alone and friendless.

When I started preschool at four years old, I had no friends. In fact, my closest companion was my mother's hand puppet called "Meep-Meep." It wasn't even an actual puppet, it was just Mom's fingers opening and closing like a mouth. But her hand became so cramped that she enlisted Dad to put an end to it.

"Where's Meep-Meep, Daddy?" I asked.

"Meep-Meep went to go live with her sister, Maude. She's not coming back. Don't look for her."

Eventually in elementary school I met a few nice girls. But I struggled to maintain those friendships, so most of the time I was on my own. There were days when I'd sit alone in the freezing snow waiting for the classes to line up, wishing recess would end. I wanted a best friend, but only one. I was terrified of groups. I decided that being alone was better than being trapped by lots of people.

I don't feel that way anymore.

Thursday, April 12

I see Beto, a boy from my ninth-period class, sitting alone at lunch today. He's a miscellaneous Social Outcast, like me. I join him. I start with a simple hello and begin eating. He doesn't talk, so I use the same approach I did with Hector.

"You don't talk much, do you?" I ask, chewing my sandwich.

He stops eating and looks at me. "I don't know you."

"My name is Maya," I say, smiling.

We sit in silence for a while, my attempts at conversation shut down. I notice frantic gestures from my choir crowd waving me over. I smile and wave back. I appreciate them looking out for me, but if I sat with them every day, I'd never meet anyone new.

I pick up my backpack and am about to leave for the library when suddenly a boy with a mustache sits down across from me. I recognize him as someone with whom I'd been in previous classes.

"Hello, again," I say to him, frantically searching my memory for his name. *I think it started with an A. Yes, that sounds right.* "I bet you don't remember me," I blurt.

"You're Maya," he says matter-of-factly.

"Oh."

"So, tell me about yourself," I say, hoping to buy enough time to remember his name.

What's-his-face leans away from me and says nothing.

"Okay, so since you won't offer up information, let me ask you questions. Are you in sports?"

"Basketball, soccer, football, and track."

Wow! A member of the Football Faction! I have unintentionally catapulted myself into sitting with a nine on the Popularity Scale.

"So, now it's my turn to ask you questions," he says.

"Shoot."

"Do you have a phone?"

"Nope," I reply. "The only person who has a cell in my family is my mom."

"Like me," says Beto, looking up from his sketch of a man on fire. Football Guy looks at Beto hard for a second and then speaks.

"Hey, Beto, could you get me . . . a milk?"

"Get it yourself," Beto hisses. Then he stands up and walks to the cooler anyway.

"Hey, can I ask you a question?" His face looks earnest.

"Sure."

What is his name? Alejandro, Abel, Adan? ADRIANO! That's it!

I'm so proud of myself for remembering that I hardly hear what he says next:

"Do you want to go out?"

My heart stops beating. My hands go cold.

WHAT?! Did I hear that right? Are you serious? Is this a joke? Did Kenzie put you up to this?

I look down at the table. They're going to have to haul me out on a stretcher from a shock-induced heart attack. Me, HOBBIT GIRL EXTRAORDINAIRE, getting asked out by someone from the Football Faction!

What do I say?

"Uhh," is the intelligent response that escapes my lips.

"Okay, Adriano," yells Beto, coming back. He's holding a stack of milk cartons. "I didn't know if you wanted chocolate milk or regular, and if you wanted regular do you want one percent or skim, so I got one of each." Beto sits down and looks back and forth between us. "Awk-ward!" he sings. "Wow, Maya, you're really red! Like a tomato!"

My hands fly to my cheeks. Sure enough, they're burning. "I think it's because I get red when I laugh! You guys are so funny, ha-ha-ha."

"You know what, Beto," says Adriano. "I changed my mind. I just want water."

Beto throws the milks at Adriano, and goes to get some water.

"So?" Adriano says.

I didn't remember your name until two minutes ago, and my parents won't let me date until May of 2000-and-never.

I am so flustered right now that I will probably pass out.

"Let me get to know you a little better first," is the best I can think of.

Beto comes back and Adriano pretends it never happened. I'm relieved, but isn't this what every girl dreams of, though, to be asked out by a popular guy? So why am I so nauseous and frightened?

Friday, April 13

Today Dad picks me up at school for a doctor's appointment. At least that's what I believe up until the moment we pull into the mall parking lot and Dad starts chuckling. He throws me my purse full of movie goodies.

"You lied."

"Not really," he says. "I *am* a doctor, and technically this is an appointment."

He laughs and opens the car door for me. That's one thing I've always loved about Dad. He never fails to treat me like a lady. Betty Cornell would approve of his manners, but I don't think that she'd like the fact that I'm skipping school to go see a movie.

Dad and I walk in and buy tickets. Even though I'm thirteen, I still hold his hand. I think that makes him smile.

We have a really great time. Dad may be a little different, but he is wonderful, funny, and gives good advice.

Betty Cornell says, *"Try telling your parents how much you love them. Let them know you appreciate all they do for you."*

"Thanks, Daddy. I love you."

He smiles. "I love you, too."

Saturday, April 14

I decide to try out a new tactic at the church bake sale tonight. Betty got me thinking.

> *It is important to remember that when you are shy it is possible for you to give people the impression that you are rude.*

I know this has definitely been true for me. Francisco told me that he was terrified of me until I talked to him, and he realized that I wasn't menacing. I'm not going to let this happen tonight.

When I arrive, I put forward my best smile. I help out in whatever ways I can. I laugh with the adults. I cut desserts. I carry plates of food around for the potluck. Eventually I don't even have to feign friendliness anymore.

I sit down next to Hector, the shy boy I befriended on Sunday. I talk for a while about everything from my aching knees to my spot in the regional choir. Then miraculously, he starts responding. His speech is soft at first, but soon he warms up and we laugh. I hear some of the girls my age whispering about us, but I don't care.

An incredible feeling of liberation settles over me.

For the first time in my life, I think people like me. And I'm seeing that it's been more than just wearing the pearls or the skirts, or even the hat (although I've had several older women come up to me and tell me how darling I look on Sundays with my hat and gloves).

So far this month, I've met so many people, and Betty's lesson is much deeper than I ever expected: I wanted popularity; I wanted other people to like me. But it turns out most people are waiting to be discovered too.

Sunday, April 15

Am I popular yet?

There's only one way to find out.

I have to ask *her* the true definition of popularity.

I'm going to find *her*. I have to tell her that more than sixty years after her book was written, someone is still following her advice. Someone out there is still listening.

I'm going to find Betty Cornell.

Wednesday, April 18

I walk into the lunchroom confident and satisfied. This morning, my orthodontist told me that I would get my braces off in four weeks! Finally!

I sit with the Spanish Club again and am much more verbal this time. After about twenty minutes I excuse myself and go to the library to finish some schoolwork. I also start to Google information about Betty. I find thousands of Betty Cornells all over the United States. How am I ever going to figure out which one is her?

Adriano follows me to the library. I was hoping to avoid him. How do I tell him I don't want to go out with him?

Adriano comes over and stares at my screen. I can't get any work done, so instead I put my backpack down on a chair and decide to shelve books. Adriano follows me and picks up a novel.

"So, what would you do if I tried to tickle you?" He nudges my side, playfully.

All right, I am now quite uncomfortable. My neck begins to burn, but I swallow and maintain my calm manner. "Honestly, I'd slap you."

"Really? . . ." Then, of all things to do, he raises his fingers and tries to tickle me. I tap him over the head with the book I'm holding. Not enough to hurt, but enough for him to get the message.

"Adriano, stop touching her!" Ms. Zaragosa, the assistant librarian says, stepping between him and me. Everyone is quiet. Ms. Zaragosa tells me to get behind the desk. I am embarrassed but incredibly grateful.

"You need to report that boy," she says, looking at me straight in the eyes. "I can show you how."

"No," I answer. "No, really, I'm okay. . . ."

The bell rings and I quickly escape the library and walk to class. Adriano trails behind.

"Boy," I say. "You nearly got yourself in trouble."

"How?"

"They want me to report you, but—"

He disappears into a group of friends.

I have a feeling that Adriano won't be asking me out again anytime soon.

I'm very relieved.

Thursday, April 19

I stand over my old lunch table and say "hi" to the gang.

"Traitor, now you come back," Francisco murmurs.

"We could compare her to Benedict Arnold, actually," says Maria, who sits studying U.S. history.

Kenzie sets her stuff down and looks at me. "She's not a traitor. She's just . . . *experimenting*." She covers her mouth. "Oh, that sounded wrong! You know what I mean. My brain's not working properly today. I can't think straight."

I pat her shoulder and walk over to the end of a table not too far from us. I've already covered most of the easy spots: Social Outcasts, Choir Geeks, Library Nerds, and Computer Geeks. Now it's time to tackle something much more difficult: an all-guy table, consisting of Band Geeks and Rich Gang Members.

As I sit down, everyone scoots away from me. When I try to start a conversation I realize that the group doesn't speak any English. The only information I get out of them is their names and even that takes forever.

Later Kenzie tells me I'm brave (and crazy) to do what I did. She's terrified of the people I sat with. She calls them *cholos* and gangsters and refuses to go near them.

But they weren't mean, they just seemed a little misunderstood.

Saturday, April 21

Dad drags me out of bed early this morning, telling me he wants to show me something "cool" on the computer. He says it's important. I mumble and groan but manage to get downstairs even though I can hardly see straight. What can be more important than sleeping in on a Saturday morning?

Dad sets me down next to the computer and scrolls onto the Facebook page of an unfamiliar woman. She's very pretty, and there are pictures of her family. Finally he pulls up an old black-and-white photo labeled "Mom and me." It's of an adorable toddler hugging her elegant mother around the neck.

"Maya, who does she look like?" he asks me, pointing to the woman.

I take a closer look. She has a classic hairdo, dark lipstick, and . . . a strand of pearls.

I let out an earsplitting scream.

"BETTY!"

. . . .

Sunday, April 22

Dear Mrs. Fadem,

My name is Maya Van Wagenen. I live in
Texas; and your mother, Betty Cornell,
has changed my life.

I know this sounds strange, but let me
explain. Years ago, my father picked
up a copy of *Betty Cornell's Teen-Age
Popularity Guide* at a thrift store. This
past summer, it was rediscovered when
we were cleaning out a closet. I flipped
through the pages, thinking that some
of the suggestions were outrageous.
But my mother had a brilliant idea. I've
always struggled socially, especially
during my previous middle school years.
I'd never even remotely considered
myself popular. My mom wondered if any
of Betty's advice from more than fifty
years ago could help me. She suggested
that for my eighth grade year I should
give it a try.

For the past several months I have worn
girdles, skirts, panty hose, and a pearl
necklace to a middle school with gangs,

pregnant teens, and frequent drug
arrests. It's had some remarkable effects.
This whole thing has changed the way
I look at people and life in general. It's
helped me grow up. It's made me laugh,
cry, and want to throw up all at once.

I've been looking for your mother,
praying that she is still alive and well.
After searching through databases and
historical records, my father found you.
It is my dream to contact your mother
and tell her what she's meant to me. I
hope you consider helping me with this
heartfelt request.

Most Sincerely,
Maya Van Wagenen

I add our phone number, hesitate, then click send, and watch the message disappear. I hug my knees. My heart is pounding in my chest. Betty's family is only an e-mail away.

Within ten minutes, the phone rings. My mom answers. Her eyes go wide and her mouth drops. She hands the receiver to me.

"Hello." The woman's voice is sweet with a faint East Coast accent, making her words soft around the edges. "Is this Maya?"

"Yes," I say. I feel my head spinning.

"This is Mrs. Fadem, and Betty Cornell is indeed my mother."

Monday, April 23

During lunch, the boy across the table from me is fuming. "Look, I don't care who you think you are, but this is a boys' table."

"I'll sit wherever I want, thank you. This is, after all, a free country," I snap back, staring directly into his dark brown eyes. I refuse to take crap from this kid. I straighten my posture and pull out my applesauce.

I'm sitting at the most crowded table in the school. It's where the less popular half of the Football Faction gather. This is also the general area where all the other guys in the school congregate. Even though I'm nervous, I'm not going to lose my ground. I am, after all, only a few days off from having to face Carlos Sanchez and the most popular people in school.

> When things go badly, you must decide not to retreat; you must attack. But you attack in a special way, not by going out and slugging the first person who comes along . . . you attack by working out your displeasure in a determined effort.

"Shut up, David. Leave the girl alone. She can do whatever she wants."

I give a grateful nod to the guy who defended me. I decide to start with him. "So," I ask, "what did you think of the exam?"

All this week we're taking statewide tests. Today it was history. Other than a few obscure questions, I think I fared pretty well. This morning Kenzie and I crammed in the lunchroom, since we aren't allowed in the library during testing. We sat side by side making up songs to help us remember the Bill of Rights.

"I know for sure that I bombed it," he says.

"Oh."

I try to make a little conversation, but they ignore me and play a game that involves guessing the scents in one another's burps.

Finally I ask the first guy, David, what his last name is.

"Why," he says, looking panicked. "Are you going to report me?"

I roll my eyes. "Yeah, like I *really* go around sitting with people so that I can report the ones I don't like."

He stares at me, thinking so hard he starts going cross-eyed. "I was being sarcastic!" I blurt, "It's a joke!"

"I don't get it," David says.

The boy sitting next to him teases, "Look, dude, she doesn't like you 'cause you're stupid. . . ."

"I never said that!" I say, but it's impossible to be heard. They decide to stick their fingers in other people's food, and try to make themselves fart.

After about ten minutes, Gabriel, a boy from my health class, looks over at me. "So," he says, "are you enjoying this?"

"The table? Well, this hasn't been the most positive reaction I've gotten."

He looks down.

"I try to be nice to people," I say. "But sometimes, they just don't understand that."

He raises his gaze and looks me in the eyes. "I'm sorry. You shouldn't listen to what people say."

I smile genuinely. "Thank you."

> ## *Maya's Popularity Tip*
> Not everyone is ready to accept a lone girl
> at a guys' table. Recognize and accept this fact,
> understanding that you may see (and smell)
> much more than you ever wanted to.

Thursday, April 26

Today, I'm sitting with a couple of Football Faction members along with a few Volleyball Girls. They have decided to completely ignored my existence. I excuse myself and go to ask Kenzie advice.

On the way, Gabriel from another table shouts over to me. "Hey, Maya, aren't you going to sit with us?"

"I'm booked today." I find myself smiling, "But don't worry. I'll be back soon."

He gives me the funny look that people have started doing whenever they're around me. I wish I could figure out what it means.

I get to our old table and see that someone's missing.

"Francisco, where did Kenzie go?"

He fidgets and doesn't meet my eyes. "She sits with Marissa now. Sorry."

I turn around to see a crowded booth overflowing with laughter. Kenzie's voice is, as always, louder than the rest. For some reason it makes me sad. I look down and sigh, realizing now how my friends might have felt when I left.

So I return to the social experiment that has become my life.

I pass by a table I sat at a couple weeks ago. One girl (a Band Geek) grabs my arm. Immediately her name jumps to mind—Lily. "Maya, you can sit with us. It's just that the people you're sitting with are mean."

I am unbelievably touched, but am still determined not to be ignored. "Thank you so much. But I can't today. Maybe later?"

She nods and the table resumes its conversation about a band trip.

I sit back down with the semi-populars but no matter how hard I try, they disregard my existence. I don't let it get me down, though. I guess they're just not willing to take a chance.

The bell rings and I walk to the door. Everyone pushes me against the glass. I'm almost sure to be crushed when 6'2" Gabriel from Monday reaches over the crowd and holds the door open for me. He smiles and I call out a thank you.

I will add him to that ever-growing list of people I've met and now consider friends.

. . . .

Thursday, 3:46 p.m. Today, I'm talking to Betty.

The phone rings and I rush to answer it, heart pounding. What if she doesn't like me? What if I say something wrong?

"Hello?"

"Hi, Maya, this is Mrs. Fadem. I'm going to put my mom on the other end, and then you two can chat. Is it okay if I listen in?"

"Of course," I say.

There's a pause, then an older woman's voice comes on. "Hello?"

"Hi, this is Maya."

"Hello, this is Betty Cornell. I think that what you did is just wonderful. I am very proud of you. So tell me a little about yourself and what you thought of my book."

I hesitate, then begin. "This past year, I've been trying out the suggestions in your book. I think it's really working."

I tell her the positive highlights of each chapter. I'm pretty sure my phone etiquette sucks because I know I say "um," "exactly," and "like" way too many times.

> ### Maya's Popularity Tip
> When you finally get to talk to your life
> teacher, mentor, and guru for the first time,
> try to make a good impression and
> refrain from squealing with joy.

I avoid telling her about all the bad things that have happened: being called names, being humiliated and mocked, and I sure as anything don't mention the girdle. Instead, I talk about the pearls.

"Don't you just love them?" she asks. "They look great on everyone. Go on, tell me more!"

I let her know that I'm sitting at different lunch tables.

"What an amazing opportunity to meet new people! Wasn't it nice, though? Did you make new friends?"

I think of my experience today. "You know, for the first time, I feel like I've got people looking out for me."

"Oh, how great! So what is coming up next?"

"Next month I'm going to go to the eighth-grade prom. Do you have any advice?"

"Is it a formal?" Mrs. Cornell asks.

"It's more . . . semiformal."

"Okay, so don't overdress. Or wear too much makeup. That's the problem. Girls try out strange hairdos and clothing that they don't know how to work with. They don't look like themselves at all. Let's see, what's your favorite color?"

"Blue," I say.

"Then you should get yourself a nice blue dress."

I smile. Her voice sounds just like I'd imagined it, gentle and matter-of-fact. I describe my family, leaving out Nat's autism and our overall strangeness. She listens enthusiastically.

"I can't tell you how grateful I am that you wrote this book. Even though it was years ago, it still rings true. It still works. It's changed my life. Suddenly I can make friends."

"You've just made my day. More than that . . . you've made my month, my year, *everything*!"

I am on top of the world.

From now on, I not only get Betty's advice from the book, but I can also get pearls of wisdom from the mouth of Mrs. Cornell herself.

Friday, April 27

Today is the day. I've been working up to this moment all month long. All year, for that matter. Today I sit with the jocks, the most popular people at our school: the highest of the Volleyball Girls and Football Faction all together at one table.

Here goes.

The bell for lunch rings, and I slowly pull myself out of my desk and drag my feet down the hall toward the cafeteria. I can hear the blood pounding against the inside of my skull. My fingers shake as I try to remember everything I've learned, what's truly important in making friends.

I sit down across from a Volleyball Girl.

"Hey, Maya, what's up?" she asks, smacking her neon-pink chewing gum.

"Hi, Cristine, can I sit here today?"

"I guess."

"Thanks."

Carlos Sanchez stumbles in with his buddy Pablo, singing "The Lion Sleeps Tonight." Badly. An onlooker would describe them as drunk, but they did the same thing during third period, so I'm not surprised.

He glances at me. I freeze and force myself to smile, even though I think I'm going to be sick.

"What's up, Maya?" He rejoins the song, then jumps back. "Holy crap! Since when do *you* sit with *us*?"

I try to stop my voice from shaking.

"I've sat with tons of people." I point to the tables around the lunchroom. The group seems impressed.

A football guy at the end of the table leans forward to see me. "Why?"

I relax a little. "For fun. Anyway, I'm moving to Georgia and—"

"WHAT! YOU'RE MOVING?!" Carlos Sanchez shouts loud enough for the entire cafeteria to hear.

"My dad got a job at a university there."

"But, you make our school look all smart and stuff. And, and now we're just gonna look dumb!"

Carlos Sanchez will miss me, too! Am I dreaming?

Some of the boys get into an argument over who will miss me most.

"No, I want to sit next to Maya."

"Too late, I was here first!"

I'm floating, honest to goodness floating! My head has to be fifty feet above the earth!

Someone from the nearby Choir Geek table hears the commotion, looks up, and sees me sitting at the most popular table at school. Her eyes widen, and she pokes one of her friends. They both gawk. One of them mouths, "What the hell?!"

I smile. Soon all the choir girls are staring at me.

I feel like a princess on a float. So I just smile and wave. The whole Popular Table is talking to me, competing, even, for my attention.

As the bell rings on another successful lunch, I get up. One of the Football Faction members leans over to me.

"Don't sit at the gangster table. They're scary."

I'm shocked at his warning. "I already sat with them. They were really nice. They just don't speak much English."

He shakes his head and disappears. When I get into the hall, all the choir girls surround me. "What were you doing?" they ask.

"I've sat with everyone. They weren't too bad."

"But the jocks are terrifying!"

"Maya, you're amazing!"

"You are so brave!"

"You've got some serious balls, man."

Wow, I mean . . . Wow. I've never been considered brave, or even bold. Now, I have "serious balls."

I practically soar down the hall to my next class, but a question keeps bringing me back to reality: Why is everyone so scared of one another?

. . . .

Still feeling the high from the cafeteria earlier today, I'm positively glowing when I arrive at a church potluck. I sit down next to Ethan, who is alone.

"Hello there," I offer.

"Hey," he murmurs. He doesn't look at me.

"Are you against being social?" I ask, teasing.

"Yeah," he remarks, sarcastically. I laugh.

I talk to him for a little while about my day, and ask about his. Then he looks at me, eye contact and everything. "Am I immature?"

"What?" I'm floored.

"Really, am I immature? Some girl told me so today, and I've never been made fun of before in my life. So, am I immature?"

I laugh. "You've never been made fun of?"

"Nope."

I pause a moment. "Then I think it's supposed to be some humbling experience sent by something greater. That, or she likes you." I smile as he blushes. "I mean it's obvious you can't get her out of your head. Sure you can be immature, but so can everyone else. I think it's good you got called out on it before you left for high school. Middle school is supposed to be a time of growth, a time to realize that you're not the only person on the planet. Sometimes it's hard to do that until someone comes along and makes you deeply ponder who you are."

"Oh. I thought everyone just respected me because I have a girlfriend."

I take a deep breath, and it's like the tension is released.

And just like that, I realize that it doesn't hurt. The crush is gone. I'm free to connect with anyone and everyone. I'm free to give honest advice from my heart.

Glory be, I am free!

"Well maybe you've got to think more about re-creating yourself," I say. "I have."

"I know. People at my school talk about you all the time. Everyone knows your name. Well, they call you 'Maya Van Woogen.'" He laughs. "They say mean things, actually: that you dress like a grandma and talk to people who don't know you. All in all you come off pretty crazy."

Ethan goes to the elite, expensive private school miles away from mine. I'm not sure how to take this. Four months ago this would've crushed me, but now, I'm more intrigued than hurt. Everyone knows my name.

Monday, April 30

Here I am again.

The lunchroom.

This is where my month first started, and this is where I choose to end it. I walk to my own Social Outcast table and sit down.

Betty Cornell says that *"Your first dance is obviously reserved for your date, as is the last."* I came with my group, and I intend to leave with them. It's almost like everything's back to normal. But not entirely. There are some key differences:

- Kenzie now sits at another table with a new friend. I suppose this is a good thing, but it makes me ache on the inside. She and I ride the bus together, though, so that's still something we share.
- Adriano deliberately avoids my gaze. I got asked

out by a Football Faction member and now he won't talk to me. But I don't care.

- I know so many more people. People I never would have spoken to if this whole experiment had never happened. It's as if there's a magnetic pull inside me toward all of humanity. It's a love that I never thought I could feel for the students I go to school with.

But there's one change that catches me off guard more than anything else. I watch as a girl tugs at her boyfriend's sleeve. He's sitting with his friends at an all-guy table, but she wants him to sit with her. It's a usual sight, but this time it plays out differently.

The boyfriend refuses, and I watch as she lets out a determined sigh. She sets down her tray among all the guys and sits down with them.

The boys look at her funny for a moment, but then just shake their heads and lower their eyes. One glances up at me.

Suddenly, I have the strangest feeling. What I did made a big difference in the smallest of ways. I opened doors. I changed what was socially acceptable, just a little bit.

I've never felt quite so powerful.

May

IT'S A DATE
& BE A HOSTESS

....

Here we are. The last month of this social experiment that came to be all because of a sixty-year-old book at the back of a closet.

I am a changed person. As I walk through the halls today, I notice how people look at me. Like I'm actually a human being, a friend even. But the biggest difference is the way I see them. I'm not scared of everybody else. For the first time in my life, I feel happy and safe at school.

But it isn't over yet. There are still two more chapters to cover in the stained pages of Betty's book: "It's a Date" and "Be a Hostess." What better way to end this year than the two hardest tasks in the book?

While we're on the subject of dating, let's discuss the history of my crushes:

My first crush was Tyler, my neighbor when my dad was in graduate school. We walked together to first grade every day. One time, he invited me over, and we played a board game in his basement.

"You're my friend, right?" he asked me.

"Yeah."

"Well, I don't want to be your friend anymore. The only way I'll talk to you ever again is if you kiss me."

I didn't want to make any hasty decisions. So, I went home and told my parents. From that day forward, Tyler had an irrational (or perhaps rational) fear of my father. Sometimes I'd throw a basketball over the fence, just so he'd throw it back. That crush lasted until third grade, when he moved away.

My next heartthrob was Blake. He was the smartest kid in the class, working on his own advanced math packets while we were still learning multiplication tables. I daydreamed about him until he started bragging to everyone that he was "so much" smarter than they were. Even back then I didn't find that attractive.

Then came Jason. Jason was in love with Vanessa, the girl who was my first encounter with real popularity. He was the most sought-after guy in our grade. Jason had a big smile, wavy brown hair, and he was picked first in every sport. I spoke to Jason one last time before we moved to Brownsville when I told him I was leaving for good. He shrugged and said, "Good-bye, Mia." He almost remembered my name. I was so happy!

My most recent and longest crush was, of course, Ethan.

I've always wondered how it must feel to like someone and have them like you back just as much. It's never happened to me (except for kiss-happy Tyler, which doesn't count). But this month the school is hosting an eighth-grade prom, and my goal is to go. With a boy. And not just any boy—someone nice. Not an Adriano.

And hopefully once I accomplish this task, I'll move into the "Be a Hostess" chapter. I have never hosted a party, but seeing that we're moving soon, it seems appropriate.

> *Responsibility is the secret of any hostess' success. By that I mean thinking ahead and planning. A party just doesn't run itself. It has to have refreshments and some sort of general scheme. And it has to have people.*

I'm going to use the fifty dollars I made during my financial month along with other money I've saved up to pay for the party. I can do refreshments. I can create a scheme. Maybe, just maybe, I can get people there, too.

Wednesday, May 2

I get moved next to a shy boy in algebra today. His name is Nicolas. He kind of looks like an extremely awkward Clark Kent: big square glasses, black hair, and beautiful brown eyes.

I smile at him as I drop my backpack and sit down. He lifts the corners of his mouth then turns around and begins talking to a friend. He has a very quiet voice and always looks faintly surprised when he's speaking.

On the way out of class, he does something few guys ever do anymore. He holds the door open and lets me pass in front of him.

There it is again, the effervescent burbling of a crush, rising to the surface. I glide to second period.

That is, until I almost crash into a couple making out.

No one wants to go to the movies and observe the antics of a loving couple in the row ahead. No one wants to go to a diner and eat a hamburger seasoned with the simpering goings-on of two moonstruck youth. The minute you go beyond holding hands in public you have gone too far. Embraces and kisses which are carried on for all the world to see are in poor taste.

I laugh. Oh, Betty, if you only knew then what the future would hold.

Thursday, May 3

"All right, boys and girls! Welcome to your first day of sex education. Today we will be going over the male and female reproductive systems. I don't want any of you to shy away from the proper anatomical terms. After that we'll watch a video on

STDs. Trust me, you'll never be the same."

Kenzie and I exchange glances. For months, Ms. Welch has mentioned sex, but it's always been broken up with food pyramid drawings and excited discussions about marijuana. Not anymore. We've been silently praying that this day would never come, and yet, here it is. Actual Sex Education with Ms. Welch.

Ms. Welch enlists a student to pass out diagrams of male and female genitalia.

"Fill in whatcha know, then we'll go over the rest."

I label all of the female anatomy just fine, but I can't figure out the *other* one.

"Ma'am, what's number twelve?" asks one boy in the back.

"Really? You don't know where your testicles are?" Ms. Welch chuckles.

I hide my face. Even I figured out that one.

Ms. Welch moves on and pushes play on the remote control.

I will not describe to you what went on in the twenty minutes following. I will, however, tell you that the film was shot in the 1980s. There were scary hairstyles, inaccurate information about AIDS, and an awful background song. It went something like this:

> *Abstinence, it means love and it means trust.*
> *Abstinence, with STDs it is a must!*
> *Why is everyone expecting me to grow up so fast?*
> *Why am I the only one who thinks relationships are meant to last?*

Ms. Welch turns off the TV.

"So, class, did you see that pus and infection? And the genital warts? That's what happens. Don't have sex. So, who wants to get me my lunch?"

I lean over to Kenzie, who has covered her eyes with her sweatshirt. "Kenzie, I think I'm going to join a convent."

"Have fun, future nun."

Friday, May 4

When I wake up and look at the calendar, I don't think about the prom, or the party, or boys, or the fact that I'm going to have to face another day of sex education.

My sister would have been eight years old today.

The realization is like a punch in the gut, leaving me gasping and holding back tears. My little sister, Ariana, would be dancing around, wanting presents and cake. Every year I wait for this anniversary to stop hurting.

I am slowly realizing that it never will.

For me, her birthdays hurt worse than her death days. Birthdays remind me of everything that will never be.

Monday, May 7

Dear Mrs. Cornell,

I was so excited to talk to you on the telephone a while back. This whole year

I've dreamed of hearing what you'd say about what I'm doing.

This last month, themed "Popular Attitude," was definitely a success. I have never forced myself to do anything as hard as talking to strangers. It has always been impossible for me to make new friends and fit into a group. Now, I know and talk to more people than I ever thought possible. I've learned that lots of people are afraid to make the first move in a conversation. Many are simply waiting for you to talk first. So many of them have wonderful stories and personalities.

I'd love your advice for this month. After much consideration I have decided to host a party. What kinds of things should I prepare? Do you know any fun games or have any ideas? What did you enjoy doing when you went to casual parties? Also, I would love to learn more about your middle school years. What were you like in eighth grade?

Your Friend,
Maya Van Wagenen

P S. Thank you so much for the modeling pictures that you sent me! They are beautiful, and I was so thrilled to get them in the mail! You have such a gift; your eyes and expressions are so bright! I can tell that you loved what you were doing. As soon as we get to our new house in Georgia this summer, I will frame them and put them on my walls!

Tuesday, May 8

This evening, the school holds an awards ceremony for students who made all As or had perfect attendance throughout the school year. I do my makeup in the car and try to get fluff off my slacks. Mom, Brodie, and Natalia choose a spot at the back of the auditorium. Dad has to teach, so he can't be there.

Up front, the eighth graders have a "Reserved" section. I sit next to a less popular Volleyball Girl. She stares at me.

Shifting, under her gaze, I decide to say, "Hi." We start chatting.

"You know," she confides, "I never respected you until I saw you sitting there, right in the middle of all those boys just chillin'. You were amazing. You just seemed so calm."

"Thanks."

She smiles at me—a genuine "I-accept-your-existence-as-a-human-being" smile.

It is the most beautiful feeling.

I turn around to look for Mom and see Dad there too. He waves. He rushed to get here between classes, just to see me. I'm incredibly touched.

After the ceremony is over I talk to Dante and then rush up to give Kenzie a big hug. Ironically, we're the only two girls wearing pants. Great minds think alike.

I can't believe the school year is almost over. But there is still so much left to do. I'm almost there, Betty.

Wednesday, May 9

Popular.

The definition was always sort of fuzzy in my head. I knew what it didn't mean. It didn't mean being picked last. It didn't mean being made fun of or having no one to sit with. It didn't mean being alone. But that isn't enough anymore. I need real opinions—am I really becoming popular thanks to Betty? It's time to start asking my peers what popularity means to them. I start with Gabriel (the tall one who rescued me from being trampled) and his table of all guys, who have been much nicer to me recently.

"Hi there," I chirp.

"You again!" says Sergio, leaning over to give me a high five.

"Yep."

Gabriel smiles. I sit across from him and pull out my lunch. One kid, Luis, scoots as far away from me as he can.

"What's wrong," asks Gabriel. "Scared of a girl?"

"Um, well, I , you see, I never know what to say around, um female types, so I, like, get nervous, and er, then I break out into hives." He shrugs and looks at me. "Sorry."

"Nice to know," I say.

They talk about girlfriends, video games, and movies. Finally I pluck up enough courage to ask, "Hey, Gabriel, I'm doing a report on popularity. What do you think it means?"

He scrunches up his forehead. "Nothing, I guess."

"Nothing?"

"Nothing. Everybody, deep down is exactly the same."

I write that down in a notebook with a star next to it.

Very interesting.

"So who do you think are the most popular people in school?" I ask.

Luis motions over to Carlos Sanchez's table. "Like, the jocks. They're um, like a bunch of bastards."

"I sat with them last week," I say casually. "They were nice to me."

His jaw drops. "You sat with them? Really? What do they talk about?"

The other guys lean in to listen.

"The same things that you guys talk about."

"No way!"

"That's impossible!"

"You're crazy!"

"It's true," I say. "You should try sitting with them sometime."

They laugh.

Thursday, May 10

I stay after school for choir practice. We're learning some choreography for our next concert. We take a break and I sit next to Eva, one of my seventh-grade buddies from the trip.

"Hi, Maya! I'm going to make up a rhyme for your name!"

"Okay," I say, laughing.

She scrunches up her nose. "Um . . . There goes Maya Van Wagenen . . . rocking my socks . . . again!"

I laugh, and Ms. Charles, the choir director, pulls out a microphone. "Okay," she says. "Who's going to audition for the solo in the song?"

Eva grabs my hand and lifts it up, "Maya will!"

I feel my face go red. I'm okay at singing, but I definitely have more of a "group voice."

"Eva, if I audition will you be happy?" I ask.

"Yes," she says, grabbing the microphone and pressing it into my shaking hands.

I sing the verse, and Ms. Charles shrugs. "I'll give it to you because it was good and it's your last year here."

"CONGRATULATIONS!" Eva yells. I blush.

The clock strikes four, and Ms. Charles tells us all to go home and rest our voices. The concert is on Tuesday and she wants us all to be healthy.

I sling my backpack over my shoulder. It really is a very sad sight. We are required to use mesh backpacks to discourage us from carrying weapons and drugs. The mesh is always tearing, leaving gaping holes in the bottom. This is my third backpack this year. My sewing kit is already stowed away in the moving boxes so I shoved quilting material in the bottom to keep my books from falling out. People snicker as I walk by, but I don't really care. I guess Betty helped me learn how to laugh at myself.

Sunday, May 13

Natalia wanders in at seven this morning and yells, *"Beep, beep, beep!"*

My sister—the human alarm clock. I sit up and glare at her. She grins widely at me and says, "Good-bye, Natalia!" She skips out and closes the door.

At least she's more courteous than she used to be.

This morning I make two invitations for the party I have planned (with Betty's prodding) for this weekend. Betty says, *"Whether you mail or telephone them, invitations should be sent out to every person you wish to include."*

I'd like to have Ethan and Hector there, which means I have to give them their invitations at church today. This is what the cards say:

BON VOYAGE!

I'm moving this summer!
You're invited to my farewell party!
Saturday, May 19
6:00 p.m.–9:00 p.m.
My house
Pizza & drinks will be served
RSVP

At church I hand one to Hector, and he looks at it for a while.

"I'm hosting a party on Saturday," I say. "You and Ethan would be the only guys from church, but it would be great if you could come."

"I can't," he says. "I have a choir trip."

"Oh," I say. I feel Ethan's invitation burning in my pocket, but I know that I won't give it to him. Ethan wouldn't come if he was the only one not from my school. What's the use?

Hector apologizes and walks away.

Monday, May 14

I'm trapped in health class, once again listening to a middle-age woman describe sex—it's something I wish I could delete from my memory. I close my eyes and try to keep the walls from closing in. Suddenly, someone knocks at the door, and I'm confident that it's an angel who has come to take me away from this horror.

"Morning, ma'am. I've come to check the students for drug possession."

"Fine by me," Ms. Welch says, smiling sweetly at the police officer.

"Empty all your pockets and leave sweaters and purses on the desks where they can be seen and easily accessed," he orders.

The officer/God-sent-creature-of-mercy leads us out of the classroom and into the hallway where a huge drug dog is waiting. He nonchalantly walks the canine down the row of students eyeing each of us carefully, then takes the dog into the room.

We're told later that two students in my grade got arrested today. Hope it's not anyone I know.

. . . .

I stay up until 11:00 making the rest of the invitations for my party. I have to admit, it isn't actually putting together the invites that takes me so long, it's coming up with the guest list. After everything that's happened, it feels strange not to include everyone. For hours I sat mulling over who I considered "most important," and it hurt. Betty says the following about those you invite:

> *A point to remember here is to be generous. Don't boycott friends you happen to be peeved with. Don't keep your list down to just the same old circle. Vary your guests.*

The list is about 70 percent choir girls, but there are the Goth Art Chicks, Nicolas (my new algebra crush, whom I plan to ask to prom), Carlos Sanchez, Kenzie, all the Social Outcasts, Dante, etc. Every time I think I'm done, I realize I've forgotten someone. I've prepared twenty-seven invitations, but I could add ten more guests in a heartbeat.

How do people host parties? It's so gut-wrenching to decide who comes and who doesn't that I feel physically ill. In light of everything I've learned so far, this kind of exclusivity just feels . . .

wrong. But alas, it's something else that I must push through.

Tuesday, May 15

Twenty-seven invitations are hidden in my backpack. I'm no longer feeling down. Instead, I've decided to just enjoy everything. Kenzie doesn't ride the bus this morning, but that's okay. I'm on top of the world! I'm also looking forward to getting my braces off during my orthodontist appointment today. Everything's finally happening! I'm feeling invincible!

I see Catalina from choir leaning against a wall in the hallway before school starts.

"Hey there, Catalina," I say. "How are you doing?"

"Good, I guess."

"Awesome. So, I'm hosting a party this weekend and would love for you to be there." I give her an invitation.

She opens the envelope and reads.

"It sounds like a lot of fun," she says. "I'd love to come to your farewell party, Maya, but I can't."

"Why?" I ask. This definitely catches me off guard.

"Allison, you know the one in our choir? She's having her birthday party that same night." She places it back into my hands. "I can't come to yours. Sorry."

My heart begins to sink, as I force the next question. "Who else is going?"

"*Everybody,*" she says. Quickly she realizes her oversight. The fact that I wasn't invited. "I mean, everybody except . . . some people."

"*It's okay, Catalina,*" I whisper. She makes an excuse and runs off. I shuffle through the stack of invitations in my hand, the majority of which are choir girls, all of whom will go to Allison's party. On the top envelope, written in big hopeful letters, is *Allison.*

I look away, trying not to cry.

I trudge through the hallway, struggling to stay optimistic. I'm not even sure if the party is going to happen, so I think about the prom. Out of the corner of my eye, I see Nicolas. My heart leaps into my throat. He's talking with a pretty Band Geek. He's laughing as he drapes his sweatshirt around her tiny shoulders. She smiles and bats her eyelashes. They hug and walk off to class together. Their hands hang at their sides, almost touching.

I shove the envelopes angrily in my mesh backpack, the quilting spilling out the sides, like the guts from a wounded animal.

My heart aches. I thought things were going to be different. I guess I've been fooling myself all along.

. . . .

After poking various instruments in my mouth, my orthodontist determines that I will be keeping my braces on for another five weeks. I won't get them off before school ends.

. . . .

The choir concert is tonight.

I hug my knees and imagine that I'm somewhere else, someone else. I now wish I'd never auditioned for the stupid solo. Who am I kidding? With my luck I'll probably fall off the stage.

Song after song is performed until it's our turn to sing our finale, "It's a Beautiful Day." If this isn't irony, what is? I remember most of my choreography, but when it's my turn to sing, my feet are like lead. Somehow I manage to walk to the microphone. I hear the CD play my introduction. I start to sing.

I try to appear happy and interested in what I'm saying, but my tongue is dry leather.

I look out into the audience. There's Dad filming the concert, Natalia with her ears covered, Brodie with a vacant expression on his face, and Mom looking hopeful.

I close my eyes and try to focus on the lyrics, but I stumble and miss a phrase. It feels as if a brick has hit my chest and it's impossible to breathe. I manage to recover enough to finish, but for me, the damage is done.

Choking on my solo

When the concert is over one of my choir friends tugs my arm. "You did super good." She snorts. "Well, at least until you messed up. The look on your face was so dumb. You messed up, like, a lot!"

"Thanks, Claire . . ." I say, looking down. A few seats away I can hear girls mocking me, singing my solo, and pretending to choke.

All of their names are written on the envelopes in my backpack.

I hold myself together until we get into the car.

"Oh, honey," Mom says. "It wasn't that bad!"

I cradle my head in my hands as hot tears run down my face.

It's not just Claire's comment that hurts. When I was in fourth grade I was an iris in the school play, *Alice in Wonderland*. I had a handful of lines. I pretended it was real, and I got into the character. People would laugh when they saw me, but I assumed it was because I was good.

On the day before the performance, I came in late to rehearsal. All the other flowers were sitting in a circle talking about something.

"And then she says her lines so stupidly! If only Maya realized that she looks like an idiot every time she opens her mouth," said the Daisy. "She's so bad at acting. . . ." Then she looked up and saw me standing in the doorway. She sneered and said my lines, exactly like I'd say them. All the other flowers laughed.

I hid in the bathroom, crying all over my sweatpants.

And now, when I look at my life, all I can see is the joke it has become. The Daisy's laughter still echoes through my head.

Is this all that my experiment has amounted to—people pretending to be my friends then being cruel when I need them most? Why did I believe I was anything but an inside joke? Carlos Sanchez was right. Kenzie was right. I'm not special, I'm just a crazy girl in Grandma shoes. I don't have balls at all.

I'm sorry, Betty Cornell. I tried.

Popularity isn't real.

I'm done.

Friday, May 18

Tuesday night as I lay in bed, I swore to myself that I'd given up on this whole popularity thing. When I dragged myself back to school the last few days, the choir girls whispered. In algebra, Nicolas asked to sit somewhere else. At lunch I didn't get invites to other tables. I just sat with my own Social Outcast group (who have now become distant). My hair was disheveled, my clothing was rumpled, and my pearls seemed out of place. Everything just hurt.

I promised I'd never write another entry.

And then it came.

Another envelope arrived in the mail this afternoon. It was from Mrs. Cornell's daughter, Betsy. In it were family photographs.

Seeing Betty as a grandmother is remarkable. Believe it or not, she looks a lot like she did in the 1940s. Her smile and bright eyes are exactly the same. In the photos, Betty is with her husband, her three children, their spouses, and nine beautiful grandkids. They look so happy.

Seeing the pictures and the neatly written letter makes me realize that I'm not alone. I've got Betty Cornell and her daughter on my side. That has to count for something.

Can I just give this all up? I've come too far, worked too hard. I guess by having everything fall apart, I forgot about all the good things that happened too.

But I don't know where to go from here.

All my confidence and inner strength—how do I find it again?

Saturday, May 19

I wake up to see the sun streaming through the window, as if it's trying to convince the occupants of our house that things will get better. It's not doing a very good job.

I finally drag my body out of bed and sit at the kitchen table trying to figure out what to do next. Since I'm not hosting my party tonight, I suppose I should deal with getting a date.

I yank a sheet of paper from the desk and absently write in big letters:

WHO TO ASK TO THE PROM

DANTE

Dante is a close guy friend. Like an older

brother, he teases me and looks out for me, but he's got someone else he adores. That leads me to the next guy.

FRANCISCO

Francisco would be fun too. But he hates school functions with a passion. I wince as I write the next name.

ADRIANO

Ugh. I scratch his name off the list.

LEON

He probably would be too shy to go. I'm afraid everyone would stand around and make fun of him for being on a date. Who am I to ask him to do that?

NICOLAS

My hand pauses as I write his name.
He's the most mature boy I know.
And sweet.
But he has a girlfriend.

I tear up the list, and lay my head on the table. My party and the prom were supposed to be the culmination of everything I've learned this year. Why is it all falling apart?

Suddenly I get that "there's-something-very-wrong-here" vibe.

Images of the last nine months play like a story through my head.

When was I closest to popularity? It wasn't when I lost weight. It wasn't when I changed my hairstyle daily. It wasn't when I stood up straight or tried new makeup or wore a skirt. It wasn't when looking at the imprints of the girdle on my thighs or when I earned money.

It was when I was talking to people. It was when I opened up my introverted circle and allowed everyone I met in. It was when I included everyone. And that's exactly what a party and a prom date do not do.

Catalina said "everybody" was invited to Allison's party.

Well, "everybody" is not accurate. Allison didn't invite me. And that hurt—a lot. By going to the prom with one person or hosting a party, that's exactly what I would be doing. It wouldn't be inclusive at all, because I'd always be excluding somebody.

Like a bolt of lightning, I see that there's another way.

My heart beats loudly in my ears and I feel like running. No. *Flying.*

I know what I have to do!

Betty Cornell, I've found my grand finale.

Monday, May 21

"Kenzie, I've had the most brilliant idea for us. If we can manage it, it will be amazing. But the only way it will work is if our hearts are really in it. Will you do this for me?"

She lifts her gaze from her phone and sighs. "Aw, this is going to be bad, isn't it?"

"No, but you have to promise to be in this with me, thick and thin."

"Whatever," she says, but as far as noncommittal phrases go, I'm glad to hear it. It's her way of consenting. I remember the day when she held me in the hallway after Mr. Lawrence died. It's impossible to think that she won't come through for me.

"Kenzie," I say, taking her by the shoulders. "I'm going to invite all the people that don't have dates to the prom on Friday to come with me." I look her straight in the eyes. "With us. Together we'll form this big, amazing group. Like the end of one of those cheesy eighties movies."

She closes her eyes and groans. She rubs her temples as if my ignorance is causing her head to ache.

"Look, Kenzie, imagine what we could do! We can change the school!" I'm practically pleading now. "You know that no one goes to the prom without a date. We can change that!"

Kenzie gasps and shakes her head. "Maya, our little hierarchy is what keeps our school from collapsing in on itself!" She lifts her hands in the air. "Those cliques are what maintain our fragile sense of order. Imagine what our lives would be like without them! It would be utter hell! If we were united, one bad person could be our downfall. I can picture it now, some kid decides to smoke pot and soon everyone follows. The groups are a means of self-preservation, dividing us from the *cholos* and gangsters. You are treading on thin ice, my friend, and believe me, these rules run deep. We are all in our right orders. Be careful what you start!"

I sigh. "Kenzie, you're such a drama queen."

She pushes her oboe case into my hands so she can smooth

back her ponytail, which became disheveled in her passionate monologue.

"Let's try, at least." I look at her, pleading. "I'm moving..." I hate to have to pull the whiny card, but sometimes it's the only thing that works. "I love these people..."

She snorts.

"It's true!" I think back to the choir girls, and I realize I'm not angry anymore. I smile at Kenzie. "There are so many kind and wonderful people out there, and I need you to watch out for them, okay? Be there for them. Show them how much you care. This is the best way to do it! We can accomplish anything!"

She mulls it over, taking her oboe case back. "Fine, just don't use my name."

"Deal. . . . So, Kenzie, will you be one of my dates to the prom?"

She pretends to gag herself. I can't stop myself from hugging her. She wipes it off.

"You rock," I say.

"Whatever."

. . . .

People who I've asked to go with me to the prom today and their responses:

- My entire Social Outcast group. Francisco took some convincing. I reminded him that I was moving and he said he might go.

- Two Goth Art Chicks. One said she wasn't going, but after I made eye contact and begged and talked it up she said she'd think about it.
- A Volleyball Girl said no, but I told her I'd wear my hair down and curl it, so she grudgingly agreed.
- One boy at Gabriel's table said no. Maybe he'll change his mind.
- A girl in English who promised to come for me.
- Beto went from "No way!" to "Possibly . . ."
- I think I got three more Choir Geeks to come, but they weren't sure.
- A girl who sits next to me in reading said no at first, but her friend and I ganged up on her, and now she has agreed.
- I asked one boy who's in choir, and he said he'd go and be part of my group.

. . . .

After school, I see Leon in the library. "Are you going to the prom?" I ask. He shakes his head.

"I don't go to dances."

"You should come," I say. "You can hang out with my group of friends, it'll be a lot of fun!"

He nods and smiles. "Thank you so much, Maya."

That's one more to add to my list.

I practically skip home.

This may seem like quite a few people, but it's still not

enough. I've got to really step it up tomorrow. And somehow I've got to get Kenzie excited about it too.

Tuesday, May 22

Once again I find myself shopping at the thrift store with Mom. Only this time it's not for Betty clothes or skirts and sweaters. This time it's for something I've never owned before.

A grown-up dress.

I've decided to follow Mrs. Cornell's advice and buy a blue dress. This ends up being much more of a challenge when Mom and I walk in and see the intimidating rows of gowns.

We begin digging through the seemingly endless racks, but everything either screams denim-clad grandma or sequined stripper. I can't seem to find any middle ground.

I run my fingers over hundreds of outfits before I see *it*.

When I try it on in the dressing room before the mirror, I hardly recognize my reflection. Mom knocks on the door and I let her in. Her eyebrows raise and she smiles. "Is this the one you want?"

"Oh yeah," I say.

Wednesday, May 23

"Maya, I think I'm gonna pee myself."

"I've got you," I say, reaching for Kenzie's hand, which is clammy and shaking. "I love all of them dearly, and I'll teach you how to as well. But first, you have to stop being scared.

They can't hurt you if you don't let them."

"I can't do this . . . how did I let myself get roped in with you?" She tries to pull away and sit back down at our safe little Social Outcast table, but I give her arm a tug and drag her forward.

"You promised, one hundred percent." By now we're rapidly approaching the first table. "Come on, it's just like we practiced."

"Maya," she says, dragging her feet as she walks, "I want something in return for this."

"Okay," I say, readying myself for some deep philosophical request.

She gulps and asks, "You know that elastic beading floss? Do you have some?"

I laugh. "Yes, Kenzie, you can have my stretchy string."

She nods her head. "All right, I'll do it."

The lunchroom is crowded, but I stopped being intimidated by all the cliques weeks ago. I sit down in the middle of the Spanish Club. Kenzie stands awkwardly off to the side, rocking from one foot to the other.

"Hey, guys, are you going to the prom? Because Kenzie and I would love it if you'd come with us and be part of our group."

They stop chewing and look up from their sandwiches. Kenzie does a strange little wave, and tries to smile. You gotta love her.

They look at each other, flabbergasted. Finally, one of them speaks.

"We'll think about it. . . ."

We go to all the other tables in the cafeteria. People can't quite comprehend what we're doing. They ask if we're desperate. They ask if we're stalkers. But we (at least I) shake off the comments and continue on. Kenzie starts out looking nauseous but after five or six tables, she warms up. Soon she's talking about our plan without prompting.

As the bell rings, I smile at her. "You did it."

"I almost threw up . . . twice!"

"Look at you, Kenzie," I laugh. "You're passing on my legacy."

She groans, but doesn't deny it as we walk off to class. Halfway down the hall she stops me. "Maya," she says, "I don't think I can come to the dance."

"What?!"

The floor falls out from under my feet.

"I just, well, um, I have a church thing."

I shake my head, trying to figure out what she's saying. "Kenzie, at the beginning of the year, you decided you were an atheist."

"I'm not going."

"Kenzie, I . . . " I try to find the words. "I need you. I even bought a dress, granted it was at a thrift store, but still . . . I need you!"

"You'll do just fine on your own." She walks off to class.

How can she just abandon me?

But before my thoughts can head down that familiar dark and scary road, I pull them back. I've done everything on this project by myself so far. I will be okay, no matter what happens.

. . . .

Thursday, May 24

This morning during algebra I open my notebook. I look down and see a page titled "Meanings of Popularity." I gasp. With all of the recent drama, I'd forgotten my quest for the real definition of that mysterious and powerful word. My heart sinks.

Then I remember. It's the eighth-grade field trip to the bowling alley today. There's still time. I pull out a pen and start asking people in my class what their definition of popularity is. We are dismissed to the buses where I continue my survey. My notebook begins to fill up.

- "To have to be the center of attention. To always put on a show."
- "Being different or out of the ordinary."
- "To fit in."
- "Being nice to people and a good student. You have friends. That's the good way, at least. The bad way is when you get popular because you pretend to be someone you're not. That's never the answer."
- "You feel comfortable in every setting."
- "People like you and everyone wants to be around you. You're looked up to and respected."
- "Everyone likes you. Everyone considers you a friend."

I then ask everyone a second question: Do you think anyone can become popular? Surprisingly, no one thinks it's impossible. I follow up with one final question: Do you consider yourself popular?

Everyone has the same answer. "No."

"Thanks," I say, to the people I interview. "Remember to come to the prom, okay? You can be part of my group."

We are all ushered into the bowling alley, the brightly painted building that witnessed the horror of one of my more painful personal faux pas: Kenzie's birthday party. While my peers are busy choosing lanes and bowling balls, I wander between tables inviting everyone to the prom and asking for their perspectives on popularity.

I start with the "unpopular" crowd.

After about an hour, I look around the bowling alley and see that I've talked to everyone except the popular people— the Volleyball Girls and Football Faction. I've received a lot of answers already, and amazingly, they all seem to be about the same. I wonder, do popular people, those who perch at the top of the social ladder, define this word the same way as those of us who are down below them looking up?

I have to find out.

Carlos Sanchez is absent, but his buddy Pablo is here, along with six others. I ask them my questions. They laugh and burst into an animated discussion on the subject.

- "Having a cool and sophisticated walk.
  You've got to be confident and sure of yourself.
  Never shy."
- "You hang out with the 'right' crowd."
- "Be cool."

"So," I pry, "do you guys think anyone can become popular?"

"Sure. Anyone can do it."

"But you shouldn't worry about it, Maya. You're super popular. Everybody knows who you are."

OH! MY! GOSH! They just used the "P" word to describe me! The most popular kids at my school just included me in the same exalted category as themselves!

I smile appreciatively, but internally my heart does a stage dive off my rib cage. I steady myself then ask my final question.

"So, do you consider yourselves the most popular people at school?"

This question seems to make them uncomfortable.

"Well, um, not the most."

"Up toward the top, but not the best."

"No, not really."

What?

In this moment it feels like the entire social ladder comes tumbling down. Had I been giving it power by believing in it so strongly? "Popular" was just a word. "Popular" did nothing to sum up all the wonderful, interesting, and amazing people I'd met.

All at once I realize that there is no ladder.

We are all the same.

As I say good-bye and leave their table, I notice that they're still talking about the subject, sharing their views on what it would take to make someone known.

I find Nicolas, my latest disappointing crush, sitting alone at a table and I join him, exhausted. Around me, I keep hearing that word. Everybody's talking about it: popularity. It fills the already blasting bowling alley, and lines every set of lips.

"So, did anybody answer 'yes' to that last question?" he asks.

I look up at Nicolas and find myself smiling. I'd noticed that he'd been paying attention to my interviews. "No. Unbelievable, right?"

"You know," he ponders, "I'd never even thought about this stuff until you came and talked to me about it. I realize now that it's more of a mindset than I'd imagined."

A boy sits down across from us. I can't help but ask him my questions too.

"I guess," he says after a moment of thought, "the only way to be popular is to do something dangerous . . . and scary. Something that no one else is willing to do."

That statement completely describes my life. That is exactly what I've been doing since September!

Just then one of the teachers calls out and tells us that it's time to go. Nicolas looks at me and we walk out toward the bus.

When we get back to school, he holds the door open for me. I smile.

"Hey, Nicolas, are you going to the prom?" I ask, feeling the hope in my voice rise. "You could always come and hang out with me."

"Who are you going with?" he questions.

I'm about to say nobody, but then I realize that it's not the truth at all. "Everyone," I confess, and I mean it.

He looks down at the ground and pushes his glasses up his nose. "I can't," he says, and walks quickly away, staring down at the ground.

There's nothing left to say.

. . . .

If you dance very badly, take lessons. A girl who must constantly excuse herself for treading on her partner's toes will not be asked to dance often. Boys are pretty fussy about such things. Though they may dance badly themselves, they expect a girl to dance well. It may be unfair, but it's true.

Due to my lack of coordination, I've decided that this is advice I really need to take. Mom is an amazing dancer, so I ask her to help me.

"I'd be glad to, Maya." She smiles and starts some moves she learned from her Zumba class at the gym. I avert my eyes until I'm positive she's stopped.

"I don't think that you honestly want me to dance like that in front of people. I'm pretty sure Dad would kill me."

She instructs me on how to step in time to fast songs. "You have to listen to the beat." Brodie watches, holding his latest LEGO creation, but he's so hyper that it's almost impossible to teach him. He's far too busy jumping around to notice that each song has its own tempo. His dancing is very *innovative*, though. I'll give him that. Mom shows me how to not only move my feet, but my arms also. "Stay loose, feel the music." I don't feel anything but the awkwardness. We practice for a few more songs when she decides to change tactics.

"All right, now I'm going to teach you how to slow dance. Brodie, put your right hand on her waist . . . no, your other right. There you go!"

"Mom! He's eye level with my boobs! You have no idea how embarrassing this is."

"Maya," Mom sighs with her hands on her hips, "you may have to dance with shorter boys sometimes in your life. It's good to start young."

I groan, but then realize that I should be breaking in the (already broken in) strappy white heels I bought at the thrift store. I rush to my room and put them on. They make it kind of hard to walk, but are still nice. I strut back and forth down the hall until I'm confident I won't fall and kill myself. I hear the front door open and realize that Dad's home.

When I get back to my parents' room, Mom, Brodie, Dad, and a buck-naked Natalia (don't ask), are all dancing around in a circle singing "Single Ladies."

Friday, May 25

A pretty dress . . . tiny slippers, a sparkling jewel,
tidy white gloves, all these laid out on the bed are
a sure sign that there's a big dance in the offing.
There's excitement in the air and the rustle of
tissue paper. The bathroom is damp with steam—

*you've never been cleaner in your life. It's hard
to believe that after waiting so long, the evening
has come at last.*

Betty Cornell's words from so many years ago still sum it up beautifully.

My dress, now hung over the counter in the bathroom, feels almost intimidating. I scrub my hair and avoid looking at it. I do two rounds of shampoo, just like many months ago. I scrub and scrub until my locks lose their greasy appearance and become soft and smooth. I rinse and ignore the growling of my stomach. I've been following the diet again, which means I haven't touched a between-meal snack or dessert all week.

Mom curls my hair so that it falls in waves down my shoulders. She makes jokes about my quiet mood, and tells me how pretty I look. I smile, but secretly my heart is pounding. It's hard to keep the doubts from worming into my mind. Why didn't I do the party? It's going to be ten times harder to go to the prom by myself and ask people to "groove" with me. And what if no one I invited comes? What if I'm the only one there without a date?

I wash my face and close the pores with ice. Then I add powder. Mom begs to do my eye makeup, so I let her. But just a little, because of Betty's advice. I apply some shiny lip gloss and brush the soft curls away from my face.

This is it.

Carefully I pull my dress over my shoulders. Then I look in the mirror.

I don't recognize myself.

Leaving for the dance

My legs seem to be ten times longer and leaner in my rounded, white heels. My shoulders and arms don't feel hairy or ugly, only willowy and graceful. And the dress! It's a light, sleeveless shift with a low neckline in a shimmery, powder blue. It ends right above my knees, and makes me feel like I'm wearing a waterfall. Fluid and powerful. My reflection is slender, yet has curves. My hair falls around my shoulders in sophisticated waves.

I smile and notice my eyes. There seems to be a hint of

something different in them but I can't quite put my finger on it. . . .

Brodie comes running up the stairs with a package in his arms, screaming nonsense at the top of his lungs.

"Ma, ya, she [gasp] she, wrote [gasp] envelope, Betty [gasp]!"

I snatch it out of his hands and tear through the tape like a ravenous beast. It is, indeed, a message from Betty Cornell.

> *Dear Maya,*
>
> *I received your letter and your picture. You look just as I imagined you from your writing. . . .*
>
> *My middle school years . . . I was just like you and your friends, with fears of entering a new world with new rules, new teachers, and so many new students and not knowing so many of them. Like you, I made myself speak to new students, joined different clubs. . . .*
>
> *You are to be commended for helping other girls come out of their shells. These girls will remember your kindness. Keep up your great work. I am anxious to hear about your party and your pearls.*
>
> *Sincerely,*
> *Betty Cornell*

I hold the letter to my chest and suddenly I don't feel so scared. I'm not alone. Betty Cornell, the woman who changed my life, will be with me in spirit, even if nobody else shows up.

Brodie reappears, standing in the doorway. I notice he's dripping wet.

"What happened?" I ask, still clinging to the letter.

"Dad and I are washing the car so that you get to go to your dance *in style.*"

I find myself smiling. "You are wonderful."

"It was Dad's idea." He looks me up and down and whistles. "You look nice. It's like Betty Cornell blessed you herself."

"Thanks, Brodie. For everything."

He grins and runs back down the stairs.

I reach for my glasses, but then stop. I can see well enough without them. Besides, I don't need any excuse to hide.

I clasp my string of pearls at my throat and drape the thin white shawl around my shoulders. I take one last look in the mirror and for the first time in my entire life, I feel . . . beautiful.

Mom takes some pictures and wraps me up in a big hug. I can feel I'm quite a bit taller than she is, especially in my new shoes.

"I love you, Maya. Whatever happens, I'm so proud of you."

She walks me out to the sparkling Chevy Malibu, and Dad opens the car door for me. In five minutes I am there, in front of the school. Dad is smiling at me, asking if I want him to walk me in.

"If only I'd had time to change, then maybe . . ." He looks down at his baggy shirt and exercise shorts. "I just feel like I'm one step behind, you know."

I love his awkward mannerisms so dearly.

"Daddy, you *washed the car* for me."

"I know, but still . . . if we'd waited just a little bit longer I could come in with you."

"I love you so much, but I've got to do this on my own."

He nods. "Okay. My parents dropped me off at my first dance too. Granted I was so nervous that I threw up on the way over and my breath smelled like puke. I don't think you'll have the same experience, though."

Feeling nauseous I change the subject. "Maybe I should've hosted a big party. It would've been easier than this. I'm going to have to include everyone, and I'm so scared."

"You're growing up so fast." He smiles. "You look beautiful, Maya. This was the right thing to do." He gives me a kiss on the cheek.

I hug him so tight it hurts. Then, I close the door.

I walk to the cafeteria to face my destiny.

. . . .

Flashing red and green lights from the stage are the only things I can make out in the dark room until my eyes adjust. The music is deafening, and I stumble about in my heels, not quite sure where I am. All of a sudden a cluster of girls I'd convinced to come as part of my group rush up to me. It's the Goth Art Chicks.

"I didn't even recognize you," one says. "You look amazing!"

I laugh, thrilled that they actually came.

I smile and return their compliments. I am now able to see a completely clear floor. No one is dancing.

I talk with the girls for a while before I ask them to dance with me.

"No way! We'll go when everyone else does."

"I'm too scared!"

Then a crowd of people abducts me from behind. I'm greeted with several customary kisses on the cheek.

It takes a minute to realize it's the Volleyball Girls, who've abandoned their dates in the corner.

"Wow, Maya, you look great!"

"You too," I say. "Do any of you guys want to dance?"

"NO! We'll go when there are more people out there."

"Oh," I say. There are only about twenty people here so far. I go around asking them to dance with me, with or without their dates. Everyone declines my offer. I continue to make the rounds until I'm back with the group of Goth Art Chicks.

That's when I notice, one girl is standing by herself, tapping her foot, and mouthing the words to the song. I don't know her, but I recognize her as one of the many strangers I invited to come with me.

I take her hand and drag her to the dance floor. She blushes, but smiles. We're the first and only people dancing. I start swaying side to side, moving my arms like Mom taught me. The girl and I twirl around a little, laughing. Tentatively, all the other girls I invited join us and we create a giggling circle. I leave the group to grab more people and bring them out to be with us. At first they shake their heads, but eventually they comply. A few guys see me dancing with their dates and come to join us too. A steady stream of people follows.

I feel blisters starting to form on my toes, but I ignore them. I focus only on being inclusive, savoring the moment.

Then I notice a boy sitting alone, staring at the ground. I tie my shawl around my shoulders and think of all those people's responses to my questions.

"To be popular you've got to talk to everybody," one girl had said. I know what it's like to be left out. I don't want his experience tonight to be the same.

"Hey!" I shout, the only way to be heard. "Do you want to dance with me?"

He shrugs and halfheartedly shakes his head.

"Come on," I say, and take his hand. He pushes me away. "No."

I step back, "All right." I suppose not everyone's ready for it.

After getting the same reaction from three or four other guys, I walk back to the floor. I dance with some more girls, bringing them out from the shadows and into the flashing neon lights. They laugh and joke. I get more compliments than I can count.

I find my way back to the group of Goth Art Chicks. Now girls grab my hands and invite me to dance. I feel a tap on my shoulder.

"You know, I wonder why my date is dancing with other people."

"KENZIE!" I shout, and hug her so hard that she stumbles back. We giggle. "You came!"

"Yeah, you kind of made me," she says, straightening the black wrap over her bare shoulders. "You look so pretty," I say. She steps back and looks at me, her head cocked to one side. "Damn girl, you need to get me the name of that thrift store."

I smile so big it hurts. Then I grab her hands.

"What are you doing?" she protests. "I don't know how to dance."

"Do you think I do?"

"No."

"Do you think I care?"

"All right," she says, and we shake our shoulders dancing right in front of the speakers. I'm positive I'll go deaf.

Then out of the corner of my eye, I see the shyest girl in school has arrived. Olivia, one of the members of our Social Outcast table, is standing alone at the edge of the dance floor. I rush to greet her. In spite of my invitation to join me tonight, I didn't think she'd actually come.

"Olivia," I say when I reach her. "Will you dance with me?"

She ducks her head down and stares at the floor. Then she nods. I smile and take her hands in mine and we twirl and spin and laugh like nobody is watching.

In my head I hear Mrs. Cornell's words from my letter: *You are to be commended for helping other girls come out of their shells. These girls will remember your kindness. Keep up your great work.*

A great work. As I see Olivia smile and laugh I begin to believe it.

Olivia, Kenzie, and I dance and dance until the music stops mid-song.

The principal grabs a microphone. "Well, it's seven o'clock everybody. It's time for you to go home. Have a great summer and a great life. We won't be seeing you next year."

Slowly, as if waking up from a dream, we all walk out into the fading sunlight. I remember Betty's words, *"On saying good night to your date, tell him what fun you've had. Make him feel that you've really, truly enjoyed yourself. . . . Let him know you're appreciative."*

Kenzie gives me a hug. "Thanks so much for coming," I say. "It meant everything to me."

As Mom and I drive away, she asks, "How was it?"

I think about everyone I danced with. All the guys and girls I pulled out onto the floor, making them part of one big group.

"Fun . . ." I say.

But then I remember all the people I invited who never showed up. I find myself missing them, wishing they'd shared in the magic.

". . . And sad." I look out the window at the passing cars.

When I get home, I brush out my curls and take off my makeup. Surprisingly, I still feel pretty. Not enchanting, but pretty.

I'm about to turn off the bathroom light, when suddenly I catch sight of my eyes in the mirror. A few hours ago, I had no idea what it was that made them look different. Now it's undeniable. Deep within their dark brown depths I see something I never have before—strength, bravery, confidence . . . and fire.

No matter what happens from here on out, there will be no more fear.

Thursday, May 31

It's the afternoon of the last day of school. I sit next to Kenzie as we ride the bus home together one final time. The heat and humidity are almost unbearable.

She smiles at me, but I can see there are tears in her eyes. I speak the words on both our minds: "Gosh, it's gone by fast."

She laughs humorlessly and bites her lip. "Hey," she says. "Let me see what everyone wrote in your yearbook."

I open it up. There are signatures on every page, crammed for space in the margins. Kenzie whistles, impressed.

"Kenzie, do you ever feel like you'll be forgotten?" I ask. "It's just, I've been thinking, hoping that I did more than just survive middle school, but somehow left a mark."

Her eyes open quickly. "You got a pen?"

"Yeah," I say, pulling one from my backpack. She snatches it from my hands and leans over the seat in front of us. I watch her, openmouthed.

"Look away, Maya, stop making it so obvious!" She purses her lips and concentrates. "There!" She sits back, admiring her handiwork. "I'm done. . . ."

I lean over and see what she's written.

M. V. & K. H.

BFFL

I laugh. "You're not the only one who wrote on school property."

She raises her eyebrows. "What do you mean?"

"I wrote on the wall in the girls' bathroom. In one of the stalls. My message is somewhere above 'Screw You, Britney.'"

"Nice. What did you say exactly?"

"Something I hope is worth remembering."

Kenzie rests her head on my shoulder as we look out the window at the cars going by. We both smile.

"We did it," she says.

"Yes, we did," I whisper, thinking back to the message I left in the bathroom stall—small and insignificant, yet the summation of the lessons I learned this year:

Real popularity is taking the time to love others, reaching out, and never being afraid to be the first one dancing.
REMEMBER THE GIRL IN PEARLS

. . . .

~ *Maya's Final Popularity Tip* ~

Popularity is more than looks. It's not clothes, hair, or even possessions. When we let go of these labels, we see how flimsy and relative they actually are. Real popularity is kindness and acceptance. It is about who you are, and how you treat others.

What began as a quirky social experiment taught me more than I ever thought possible.

All the times that I felt popular were because I had reached out to other people. I remember helping Isabella on the choir trip, Valentine's Day, sitting at all the different lunch tables, and the prom. If we forget that connection, we forget what it truly means to be popular.

Do I think anyone can do it? Absolutely.

But it's not easy. You have to be strong. You have to love people for who they are. After you move beyond the girdle, the white gloves, and pearls, Betty Cornell really understood this principle.

Maybe you ask, what has this all got to do with popularity? The answer is that popularity depends on your ability to get along with people, all kinds of people, and the better you learn to adjust to each situation the more easily you will make friends. You will find that you can make those adjustments more successfully if you have yourself well in hand. And the only way to get yourself in hand is to know yourself, to analyze yourself, to turn yourself inside and out as you would an old pocketbook—shake out the dust and tidy up the contents.

We can bring about a lot of change on this planet (and in our schools) by digging deep, finding our best selves, and shining that light of compassion. If we become afraid of what may happen or worry what others may think, it's easy to forget what's most important.

The world is a very big place that needs more caring. Imagine what would happen if we were all *truly* popular. If we all *truly* loved.

This year I was laughed at, I was praised. I was ridiculed, I was complimented. I was left out, I was included. But through it all, I was fortunate enough to learn and experience the real definition of that all-elusive word.

I, Maya Van Wagenen, became popular.

Epilogue

∙∙∙

Wednesday, August 1

There they are, the pearls, thumping against my neck as I hurry up the stairs. My knee screams in protest, and I can't help wondering what kind of person builds a high school on a hill. I'm grateful not to be wearing my girdle anymore. Imagine the chafing.

It's lunchtime already on the first day of my new school in Georgia, and I wave at a friend I met this morning, a senior named Esme.

"You can sit with me, if you like . . ." she says when I walk over to her.

"I'd love that, thank you."

She smiles and we sit down at a table. I pull out my lunch,

a cheese sandwich on whole wheat bread with a bag of grapes. I think about my diet almost a year ago. This would have been very appropriate.

My hair is cut shorter now, and hardly reaches my shoulders. It's still long enough to pull back into a stubby ponytail, but when it's down (like it is today) I don't mind it as much as I used to.

I sit up straight as Esme tells me about herself and the school. Posture is not as hard as it was in November, but I still have to think about it.

I'm wearing makeup today. I've almost run out of the original stuff Mom and I bought at the grocery store at the beginning of December, but I managed to scrape the last bit of powder out of the container this morning, after I'd put on my clothes. Freed from the constraints of a school uniform, I'm wearing a knee-length skirt with a blue blouse and a black sweater, along with my ballet flats. My whole outfit is tidy, and I've sprayed on some perfume.

Suddenly, I notice a girl who sits by herself at a table, looking completely out of place. She leans over her lunch tray and stirs her mashed potatoes. Without hesitation I excuse myself and walk over.

In that moment I don't know about all the people I'm still going to meet this year. I don't know about the girl in my drama class whose laid-back sense of humor and child-like excitement remind me of a certain best friend. I haven't yet introduced myself to the boy whose intelligent wit and impeccable manners are comparable to that of a certain crush who sat next to me in algebra. I haven't heard the words "Hey, Maya" come from the basketball player who is unmistakably similar to a certain guy who wanted to read a book about gay pigeons.

The only thing I know right now as I walk up to this girl sitting alone in the cafeteria of my new school is what Betty Cornell taught me to say last year:

"Hi, I'm Maya."

My family in Georgia

ACKNOWLEDGMENTS

I am infinitely grateful for all of the wonderful people I have had the opportunity to meet and work with during the course of writing and publishing this book. The journey from rant-filled journal to polished manuscript was a powerful one, and I couldn't imagine making it without the assistance and support of so many.

I would like to thank Margaret Stohl—for her constant willingness to help, her advice, and her friendship—as well as Stephan Pastis, for reading that original manuscript and thinking enough of it to pass it on. Also, I owe a lot to Nick Staller and Ryan Hermosura, who believed in the message of the book strongly enough to drop everything and promote it. Shout out to the Hardys and Montoyas for their encouragement and for keeping the secret.

Then of course, I must mention my outstanding publishing people. I would like to thank Dani Calotta, for creating such a beautiful book design and allowing me to be part of the process that breathed life into the pages. Deborah Kaplan was a spectacular, fun, and generous art director (thank you for the clothes!). Rosanne Lauer saved my (four) bum(s) with her mad copyediting skills by catching mistakes many sets of eyes had missed. I am extremely grateful for Elyse Marshall who kept me from getting lost, rocks high heels, is an amazing friend, and still finds time to be the world's best publicist. Julie Strauss-Gabel did breathtaking work as editor, sent me books (yay books!), and helped me grow as a writer. It was so much fun to work with her and see her vision for the manuscript from the very beginning. And she was right, Penguin does have the cutest logo. Thank you to my entire kick-butt Penguin family (which is pretty much the coolest bunch of people ever).

Lucy Stilla helped to bring the story to a whole new audience, and Cecilia de la Campa is working to get *Popular* all over the globe. It's been a dream come true seeing that my work will be published in places I have always dreamed of visiting. Daniel Lazar, my phenomenal agent, deserves a standing ovation for always going above and beyond, replying to e-mails and phone calls pretty much 24/7, and being there for me every step of the process. Plus he's a great editor and an awesome person.

I am so grateful for all the teachers who pushed me to be better, helped me to improve, and inspired me to dream. This started early with Ms. Hunter, the elementary school teacher who taught me how much fun literature could be. Ms. Corbeil helped me survive those last two years of middle school. Librarians do change the world, one book recommendation at a time. And of course Mr. Lawrence who gave his best to me and all of his students. Every time I sit down at my computer, I strive to prove him right.

The Statesboro community has been overflowing in their support and enthusiasm. Although I am not a Georgia girl by birth, they have made me feel incredibly welcome and loved. I would also like to voice my appreciation for my fantastic uncle Eric Van Wagenen, who was always just a phone call away. Without him, I never would have had the courage to go about getting this published. My grandparents Richard and Sherry Van Wagenen were also incredibly helpful, by taking me out of the will every time I failed to produce the next chapter. It was their impatient phone calls, loving threats, and phenomenal pep talks that kept me writing in my most frustrated moments. My love goes out to all of my glorious aunts, uncles, cousins, grandparents, and great-grandparents who read the manuscript, sent pictures, and shared in this part of my life. My heart is full of appreciation for Betsy and Bruce Fadem, as well, who welcomed me as part of their family.

I appreciate my wonderful siblings: loving Brodie, funny Natalia, and sweet Ariana, for their profound influence on my life. I am indebted to Michael Scott Van Wagenen, my father, for finding the book and never getting rid of it, for locating Betty, and for being there with support and advice whenever I needed it. Thanks to Monica Delgado Van Wagenen, my mother, for coming up with the idea and spending so many hours reading and discussing with me (even at three o'clock in the morning). I am truly blessed with a wonderful set of parents.

I am so grateful to the many students at my school, who are the very real characters behind this story. I am so happy to have had that time in Brownsville, Texas. This adventure couldn't have unfolded like it did anywhere else.

And thank you, Betty Cornell.
Thank you for everything.

Republished and available
for a whole new generation of readers,
the 1950s popularity guide that inspired
Maya Van Wagenen's *Popular*!

Available now!